Praise for *How You Do . . . What You Do*

"Bob Livingston and I have been business associates and friends for more than 40 years. Bob's years as a senior executive with Lipton and as a consultant have given him the opportunity to observe many companies in their pursuit of Service Excellence. With his natural good humor and strong integrity, Bob brings a unique approach to achieving Service Excellence. Now he has reached the position in life where he can share what he has learned. With *How You Do . . . What You Do*, Bob shares his experience and knowledge and shows readers how they can be more effective in their jobs and life."

—Nick D'Agostino
Chairman and Chief Executive Officer
D'Agostino Supermarkets

"*How You Do . . . What You Do*'s messages are grounded in the reality of business. Bob Livingston's ideas do not come from a classroom; they come from real-life experiences that make or break a business plan—and a business. Rather than his teachings being validated by academia, they have been confirmed by his accomplishments in many business environments—the places where it counts. Anybody who wants to understand the competitive advantages that come from a service mentality needs to read this book."

—Art Drogue
Senior Vice President Customer Development
Unilever USA

"Bob Livingston is the single best client person I have ever met. He has defined great service in every endeavor over an illustrious career. It is not just his passion for complete client satisfaction that sets him apart but the focus and discipline that underlies his approach to service. This book showcases the full range of skills, strategies, and commitments that are required to become a top-performing service organization. *How You Do . . . What You Do* is an inspirational and great teaching book."

—John J. Lewis
President, ACNielsen North America
The Nielsen Company

"With a fragmented customer and retail network and a laser-focused cost obsession, customer service has sadly waned from today's marketplace. *How You Do . . . What You Do* grounds us in why and how we can recapture the magic of delighting our customers. Bob's extensive experience with retailers and brokers and with leading large sales teams has framed his passion and focus and validates how service wins in today's marketplace. *How You Do . . . What You Do* is a great read with immediate application!"

Duncan Mac Naughton
Executive Vice President
SUPERVALU

"The principles Bob addresses in *How You Do . . . What You Do* as they relate to building loyalty certainly apply to what I do as well. A loyal following of fans is what every artist strives to build and maintain. How I do what I do determines how successful I am. There are great lessons in this book that apply to everyone, regardless of his or her career. It is a wonderful read."

Brad Paisley
Country Music Artist

"*How You Do . . . What You Do* perfectly describes the reality that surrounds service and what it takes to get Service Excellence right. What you will find in Bob Livingston's book is a simple method for implementing world-class service that will grow any business. There are no complicated theories because that is not what service is about. Instead, Bob offers straight talk that can immediately be applied to your business. Read this book and you will get a thousandfold return on your investment.

—Steve Schmidt
Chief Executive Officer
Office Depot Business Solutions

"It is impossible to know Bob or read his words and not know that he has an intense and unshakable passion for service. As an associate of CROSSMARK, I have had the pleasure to experience first hand the insights and reflections Bob has captured in *How You Do . . . What You Do*. If you will allow just a measure of Bob's passion and knowledge to impact your life, you will be on your way to providing service that clients truly appreciate."

—John Thompson
Chief Operating Officer
CROSSMARK

How
you do ...
What
you do

Bob Livingston

CREATE SERVICE EXCELLENCE
THAT WINS CLIENTS FOR LIFE

How
you do ...
What
you do

BOB LIVINGSTON

New York   Chicago   San Francisco   Lisbon   London
Madrid   Mexico City   Milan   New Delhi   San Juan
Seoul   Singapore   Sydney   Toronto

1 2 3 4 5 6 7 8 9 0   DOC/DOC   0 9 8

ISBN 978-0-07-159278-9
MHID 0-07-159278-4

McGraw-Hill books are available at special quantity discounts to use as premiums and sales promotions, or for use in corporate training programs. To contact a representative, please visit the Contact Us pages at www.mhprofessional.com.

This book is printed on acid-free paper.

Library of Congress Cataloging-in-Publication Data
Livingston, Bob.
    How you do—what you do: create service excellence that wins clients for life / by Bob Livingston.
       p. cm.
    Includes index.
    ISBN 978-0-07-159278-9 (alk. paper)
1. Customer services.   2. Customer relations.   I. Title.
    HF5415.5.L585 2008
    658.8'12—dc22

                                                                   2008011683

Dedicated to the Excellent Service People Everywhere;
you know who you are!

Contents

Foreword

Remember the old adage that "the customer is always right"? It is as true today as ever. But in this increasingly digital economy, customers also are in control; and they are challenging businesses of all stripes to identify their wants and needs and then meet, and even surpass, them time and again.

It still surprises me how many companies have yet to take up the challenge. As I go about my personal and professional lives, I'm struck by the lack of attention and, at times, apparent indifference to the client or customer experience. I don't know if it is intentional. I cannot believe that it would be the case. I do know, however, that in one way or another, it comes at a considerable cost.

Throughout my career, I have always identified with individuals and organizations who believe in creating great client experiences. During my tenure at GE, where I oversaw businesses as diverse as jet engines, water-treatment systems, financial services, lighting, and plastics, the common denominator was the ability to understand what was important to customers—even if, sometimes, they didn't yet realize it themselves—and the willingness to do whatever was necessary to service those needs. At GE Rail, for example, we didn't simply build and sell the most advanced locomotives; we also helped railroads take advantage of technology to enhance the ways they served their own customers.

How you do what you do, as Bob details it throughout this book, is an incisive capture of this notion. In this era of unrelenting change, competitive differentiation comes in a variety of forms, whether it is highly developed innovation, superior technology, sophisticated communications, or greater information accessibility. But as we continually innovate, adjust, modify, and improve, invariably things go wrong. We miss deadlines or milestones. Our promises fall short of expectations. Our competitors attempt to "one-up us," and at times they succeed.

What then do we have in place to save the day?

No matter how much businesses and markets change, the one constant that remains is the relationships we maintain with our customers and clients. In any given week, we as consumers interact with myriad companies, products, and services. We are quick to assess how effectively they satisfy our "hard needs." Yet we also judge, consciously or even subconsciously, how well they do what they do. If a company's product or service doesn't measure up to our standards—or they fail to deliver or support their product or service to our satisfaction—more often than not, we can easily go elsewhere. Each of us has that power.

Is it any different when businesses serve other businesses? Not really.

In 2006, I became chairman and CEO of The Nielsen Company. As the world's leading provider of marketing information, audience measurement, and business media products and services, we have a front-row seat at the ongoing interaction between companies and their customers. And by tracking consumer activity from concept to consumption, we have developed an extremely wide-angle lens on issues important to our clients.

At Nielsen, we are transforming ourselves into a single, streamlined company by consolidating our global business services and working more directly with clients to provide the right solutions. The shorthand version: simple, open, integrated.

We can do more for our clients by operating as an integrated company than we could if we continued to function as a collection of individual businesses. We can rapidly deploy best practices. We can eliminate activities that don't contribute to clients' success. And we can put more resources where they are most needed. As a result, we have greater opportunities to grow our own revenue and earnings.

The benefits of continually focusing on the customer are evident. So is the harm in failing to do so.

In a marketplace where the number of new products every year has soared, consumers have more choices than ever before. The result is greater brand fragmentation, making it essential to put more support behind products to gain and maintain long-term customer relations.

Consumers also have the technological means to share their likes and dislikes with people they know and don't know. Our own research shows that despite the expanding array of marketing platforms and sources, consumers still place the highest level of trust in other consumers. New digital media allow consumers to assess other consumers' reactions directly via "buzz."

Service Excellence isn't just a best practice. It also has to be an intrinsic value for any company that hopes to succeed in this highly competitive environment.

During his career as a sales executive at Unilever, and now as I observe him in serving as a consultant to The Nielsen Company, Bob Livingston's passion for Service Excellence is clear to everyone with whom he interacts. It is equally apparent in this book.

How You Do . . . What You Do is a compelling approach to a service strategy that is simple in design, easy to read, and an end-to-end solution. Loyalty can be the earned reward for Service Excellence.

David Calhoun
Chairman and CEO, The Nielsen Company

Introduction

A Service Revolution

If you are utterly irritated by the insidious decay of service in our society, I invite you to join in the launch of a Service Revolution that is designed to improve how we interact with one another in our service relationships. If you are as disappointed as I am with how you are treated as a customer or a client, please join me in a mutiny to reverse this appalling trend.

Complaining about bad service has become a national pastime, but has the complaining diminished our crisis? Not in the least. If we want our service landscape to change, we must band together to proactively transform the people, places, and processes that are driving us to distraction. Every time I speak on the subject of service deterioration, I meet with virtually unanimous consensus about the sad state of our service relationships. And yet nothing ever changes, and no one takes any action.

I trust you are as furious as I am about how badly we are being served. How much longer do we intend to wait before we stop talking about the problem and start teaching, leading by example, and if necessary, rebelling to bring about change in the way people serve one another? Throughout this book, I ask our readers to join me in ending the era of arrogance, insolence, distraction, and egocentricity from which this decay in service stems. It is time to rebel and say, "Enough is enough." If those who provide service do not change, we will take our buying power elsewhere.

Sadly, it has come to this. If you want service to improve, you must stop agonizing about the problem and join your fellow readers in the revolution to transform *how* we serve.

In one form or another, we all serve because service relationships and roles are situational. So by transforming how *we* serve, as individuals or companies, we launch a grassroots movement that has a chance of taking hold. Consider the wisdom of the Golden Rule, "Do unto others as you would have them do unto you."

Join me by actively engaging in this book and agreeing to become a part of the Service Revolution. In laying out "how you do what you do," we offer the rationale for change. These next 14 chapters provide a roadmap for transforming yourself and, by way of these new behaviors, becoming an active leader in our Service Revolution.

This very personal crusade took form nearly 10 years ago. I had spent a 35-year career cultivating strong service relationships with clients, so as to foster their loyalty toward our products and company. This was in the time before technology, with its allure of productivity and efficiency, introduced distance and detachment into our interpersonal relationships. Not coincidentally, as technology became a more pervasive means of managing our service relationships, the quality of those relationships began to broadly decline.

Please don't misunderstand my stance on technology. There are numerous examples of ways in which technological advancements have benefited consumers and increased their levels of satisfaction. The banking industry has enabled 24/7 access to our money via ATMs and online transaction capabilities. Fast Pass has reduced waiting lines at the Disney parks, thereby improving consumers' vacation experiences. These are just two instances of businesses that have implemented technological solutions to make their consumers' experiences better, faster, and cheaper. However, many companies use technology as a means for making their *internal* processes faster and cheaper, leaving the consumer to hope the improvements will trickle through in the form of better service. And yet when things go awry, it is that same technology that can impede a resolution and create extreme service dissatisfaction. Hence, our predicament.

During recent years, the time in which so many service relationships visibly began to falter, I experienced a personal awakening. I began to experiment with possible solutions and approaches with the clients I served in my consulting practice. However, it wasn't until I worked closely with a client who shared my passion for great service that a definitive answer came to me. Together, this client and I set out on a journey to prove that there is a better way to serve. For me, the journey lasted close to four years; for them, the journey continues.

This wonderful client is a company named CROSSMARK, a large sales and marketing agency headquartered in Plano, Texas. They represent many of today's leading consumer packaged goods companies in the sale and in-store merchandising of their products to a majority of retailers across North America. This is how our journey began:

In October 2003, I presented to their Executive Management Committee the findings of a non-service-related study I had conducted on CROSSMARK's behalf. During my postmeeting debriefing with John Thompson, president of CROSSMARK Retail, I took note of an intriguing lapel pin that John was wearing, proclaiming "I Care."

When I questioned John about the origin of his pin, he explained that CROSSMARK had just launched an internal service initiative at their corporate headquarters, and the purpose of the initiative was to design ways to serve one another better. Needless to say, my passion for the art of service stimulated a great deal of curiosity about this initiative. Was the program limited to internal employees? Were clients included? What about their client-based field representatives? Was it nothing more than a slogan? I asked John a seemingly endless list of questions.

"We're focusing on only our internal service at headquarters" was John's response. That reply initiated extraordinary dialogue and study, culminating in the launch of CROSSMARK's cultural transformation program designed to give rise to a true service company. At the conclusion of numerous follow-up meetings and discussions, their board determined that the true path to Service Excellence required the participation of *everyone* in the company.

Thus, we embarked on a journey of cultural transformation that resulted in CROSSMARK achieving competitive differentiation through *Service Excellence*—what I refer to throughout this book as "*how* you do *what* you do." We were retained by this client for nearly four years for the purpose of raising every employee's level of awareness and participation in his or her service transformation. During that time we worked almost exclusively on this undertaking. In 2007, CROSSMARK assumed complete ownership of the ongoing process of "deep rooting" the new culture—and so their journey continues.

Our transformation team numbered three: I was joined by my son, Rob Livingston, who created and prepared most of the material we used during the transformation, and Jim Borders, CROSSMARK's then COO, who provided his leadership and was the company's internal champion during the early years. We conducted five separate transformation meetings at each of CROSSMARK's 30 regional offices, with each of us logging close to a half-million air miles by the end of this undertaking. As a team, we worked closely with 1,700 of CROSSMARK's key people "spreading the word," building awareness, and creating excitement for what can happen when everyone improves *how* they do *what* they do.

Throughout the chapters of this book, we will be referencing the CROSSMARK experience as a best practice for achieving differentiation through Service Excellence. That experience forms the basis of our methodology. It is the means to changing your service culture.

So if you truly want to bring an end to this service crisis, please join me in this crusade. Talking about bad service has yielded little if any improvement. Complaining about bad service has been met with deafening silence. But by behaving differently—one person at a time, one company at a time—perhaps we can transform the service landscape. Everyone wins.

In the pages that follow, I encourage you to study and learn the five steps of Service Excellence and to adopt our roadmap. As an individual or part of a company, you will find relevance in the examples and support for your rationale to join our Service Revolution. Those who serve well are reaping the rewards of loyalty today. You can too.

The solution we present in this book is simple, direct, and easy to follow, and I know of none better. I believe you will find elegance in its simplicity and ease in its implementation, and the outcome may exceed all expectations.

I ask you to ponder your only two alternatives: Will you allow the agony of poor service to prevail? Or will you join with others in our Service Revolution to transform yourself into a service zealot and to be recognized for *how* you do *what* you do?

The choice is yours.

1

The Beginning

1

The State of Service

How important is service in America? Once considered a manufacturing nation, foreign competition and the current vogue of "off-shoring" manufacturing operations have contributed to the preponderance of service companies that now fuel the U.S. economy. The U.S. government estimates that as much as 78 percent of our gross domestic product is derived from services, not products.

We have evolved into a nation of servers. The Bureau of Labor Statistics' estimates are that between 110 and 115 million people in the United States are employed in the sales and service industry. So, to answer my initial question, service is clearly very important in America. But do we do it well?

Consumers don't seem to think so, if you consider the ongoing decay in their satisfaction with service companies. The headline on *BusinessWeek*'s October 23, 2000, cover doesn't even ask the question—it flat out states "Why Service Stinks." Seven years have passed since that issue of *BusinessWeek* appeared on newsstands, but the exasperation I felt while first reading that article has only grown in these intervening years. Why? Because, much to my utter dismay, the condition of service has only continued to deteriorate further.

In fact, I have been so troubled about this worsening state of service that I felt compelled to write this book, drawing upon the many lessons I've learned on the journey of my life's work. I hope to further the level of awareness regarding our service crisis and, more importantly, offer a solution that has been proven to work for individuals, teams, and companies.

For its article, *BusinessWeek* surveyed the attitudes of consumers about vital service industries and found a six-year erosion in consumer satisfaction from which virtually no segment was spared. Particularly disconcerting for these businesses were the findings that dissatisfaction led to frustration, frustration led to anger, and angry consumers went elsewhere. As alarming as these results were, we have experienced a seemingly incessant degeneration in the state of service since the survey's publication in 2000.

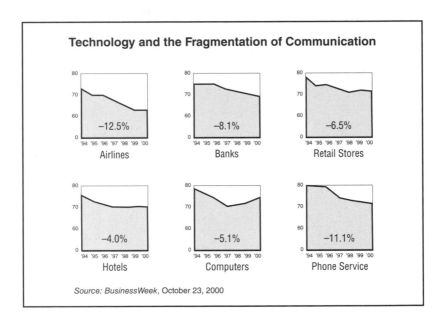

Technological developments, advancements in communication, and the Internet have, on the one hand, made the world very small. Yet the virtually limitless output from these sources has, on the other hand, made the world even bigger. With blogs, Web sites, customer relationship management (CRM) software, instant messaging, smartphones, and personal digital assistants (PDAs) come infinite opportunities to serve better. But are people really being better served? Hardly. Are these multiple communication vehicles really an improvement? Not really.

During my 30-year tenure at Unilever, I had the opportunity to work closely with two people who were exceptionally client focused: Rich Collins and Rich Maryyanek. They now run Big Tent Entertainment, a successful marketing licensing firm in New York City, and they recently shared with me how they must contend with the daily challenges of connecting with clients in this highly wired world:

"A big part of what we do is relationship based. A very big part of each day revolves around dealing with people—our clients, our colleagues, our partners, and our customers. And while we certainly make full use of the latest technology, we never let it become a barrier between us and the people we work with. We're not sure who first said it, but we subscribe to the axiom that 'very little happens from behind a desk.'"

Rich Collins, the CEO, adds, "People no longer consume media the way they used to. Just look around on any street in any town and you'll see iPods, Nintendo DS, PSPs, and multimedia mobile phones. But it's not just about the way we choose to consume media; it's equally about the brands we choose to consume. We are no longer obedient consumers, following the latest dictates of some multi-million-dollar ad campaign.

"In our opinion, the smart marketers are those who eliminate campaigns that view people as objects to be manipulated in favor of a more modern approach, one in which customer and brand are linked together in a two-way relationship. In terms of the licensing of derivative products, we believe that this activity must be seamlessly linked to the marketing strategy. Here again, a failure to recognize and understand the people who might purchase these products can lead to suboptimization or, worse, a total failure of the brand beyond its core product."

The explosion in technology and communication vehicles has significantly fragmented our means for interacting with consumers. It has made it more difficult to form live connections with people and to connect with people for uninterrupted periods of time. As a result, we are presented with some interesting challenges:

- What is the impact of the fragmentation of communication vehicles on basic service, let alone Service Excellence?
- How do you reach consumers and clients in order to develop a relationship?
- How do you sustain relationships with them in this new world?
- How can marketers and sales professionals approach this challenge?

Finding answers to these questions is far more difficult now than in the day when a formulaic approach to building client relationships was fairly effective. The number of options has soared, but communication is fragmented, and those you serve have become increasingly overtaxed, distracted, and demanding.

Technology and the Alienation of Customers

Technology is a tool; it is not a replacement for creating positive memorable experiences for customers and clients. Technology should be used to enhance customer relationships, not to create them. Unfortunately, in an ongoing effort to reduce costs, companies are utilizing technology-based customer service systems at an increasing rate, with less than positive outcomes.

Consider the example of interactive voice-recognition programs. In a study conducted by Forrester Research, 90 percent of consumers reported that they disliked this technology. Why? Technology-generated interactions are impersonal, difficult to use, and treat everyone exactly the same. And most people prefer personal attention when dealing with service issues. Customer Care Management & Consulting created the following depiction of how people's rage increases with each successively less humane system feature.

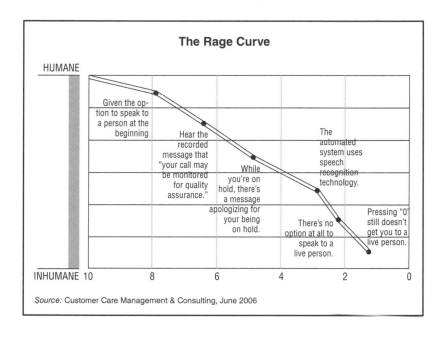

The Rage Curve

HUMANE

Given the option to speak to a person at the beginning

Hear the recorded message that "your call may be monitored for quality assurance."

While you're on hold, there's a message apologizing for your being on hold.

The automated system uses speech recognition technology.

There's no option at all to speak to a live person.

Pressing "0" still doesn't get you to a live person.

INHUMANE 10   8   6   4   2   0

Source: Customer Care Management & Consulting, June 2006

Further exacerbating these problems is an apparent reliance on technology that may be unreliable or overwrought. Forrester Research also found that more than 25 percent of customers' online questions were never answered, and industry studies have indicated that an average of 35 percent of all e-mail inquiries to companies are not responded to within seven days. Planetfeed back.com found that, of the 800,000 consumer complaints they surveyed, a full two-thirds received no response at all.

Add to this disconnect between technology and service the phenomenon of companies outsourcing their servicing responsibilities to countries where technical skills are high and labor costs are low (for example, service call centers). In the eyes of consumers, these technology-based interactions are meeting with only limited success.

For every customer-service superstar, there remain a thousand (ten thousand? a million?) losers. Day-to-day service is a string of bad blind dates, an endless series of humiliations. Three dollars a minute for technical assistance for my computer?

Comedian Lewis Black[1]

New community, social networking, and retail Web sites appear overnight. MySpace, YouTube, Facebook, Amazon, Yelp, Craigslist, and Angie's List dominate the news, but there are hundreds of others. The message is that, regardless of the business you are in, you can access instant feedback from the individuals in your target audience via their ordinary communication vehicles. If you are in the music business, MySpace and Amazon are great resources, while video businesses rely on information gleaned from YouTube and Veoh, and a small restaurant may benefit from Yelp or AmericanTowns.

The caution is that these sites can be polarizing. Those who love their experiences want to tell the world, but those with negative stories often rant even louder. The people in the middle (no doubt, more than half) may not ever say a word. Nevertheless, blogs and online social communities can provide instantaneous alerts to problems, potential concerns, likes, dislikes, new trends, and issues of customer service. Companies now have a unique opportunity to develop leading-edge products and service solutions if only they can mine the wealth of data from these new information sources. The Nielsen Company has developed sophisticated measurement and

---

1 Chuck Salter, "The Agonies of Lewis Black," *Fast Company*, September 2006.

interpretation approaches to analyze this information and design actionable solutions. This is certainly a step in the right direction.

And so despite our technological advances, it remains an incontrovertible truth that personal relationships are at the core of superior business interactions. As this new century progresses, the appalling trend in service brought to the forefront by *BusinessWeek* in the year 2000 only continues to worsen. In those companies where service is no longer taught and the emphasis is placed instead on new technologies, the paradigm must change.

Still, there is hope. Successful companies have realized that technology, used appropriately, can enhance the customer experience. Companies such as L.L.Bean, American Girl, Frontgate, and Lands' End have found a way to combine the latest in customer relationship management solutions with a team of individuals who provide the personal touch that is at the core of Service Excellence. There is a role for technology in the customer relationship, as long as it is not used as a substitute for personal connections.

> The more high tech the world becomes, the more people crave high touch solutions.
>
> John Naisbitt, *Megatrends*

The Consequences of Poor Service

Never take for granted the relationships you have built with those you serve. Complacency and disregard lead to the breakdown of a relationship, and the people you have wronged have the final word in that relationship's outcome. *They leave.*

Phil Lempert, an expert on consumer issues and the food trends editor for NBC News' *Today* show, shared these facts as to why customers leave relationships:

- 1 percent pass away.
- 3 percent move away.
- 5 percent are influenced by friends.
- 9 percent are lured away by a competitor.
- 14 percent are turned away by product dissatisfaction, *but . . .*
- *68 percent leave because of poor attitude or indifference.*

Clearly, we have little or no influence over some of the reasons relationships fail. However, the principal motivation behind customers leaving a relationship is absolutely within our control, and that is our behavior. So the question now is, if attitude and behavior are the predominant reasons relationships fail and we have complete control over our behavior, why do we jeopardize our relationships time and again?

It is not that people don't care about relationships and don't consider Service Excellence their job. Nor is it that they are unwilling to make sacrifices, put other people first, or go out of their way to ensure flawless execution of the service chain. It is simply that they do not appreciate the significance that their interactions may have on the person or client they are serving.

At times, it seems as if Service Excellence is simply impossible to achieve, despite the good intentions of those who serve. Yet some companies do achieve it. In fact, the people and companies who "get it" appear to practice Service Excellence with ease as part of their daily routine. How do they do this?

Before embarking on this journey to discover just how uncomplicated it is to practice Service Excellence, consider the magnitude and rapid escalation that negative service experiences have on an individual, team, or company. When your customers perceive your lack of interest in them and become dissatisfied or disenchanted, they set a destructive tsunami in motion. I have heard the following said about dissatisfied customers, and I am paraphrasing axioms heard anonymously. Some of those comments are:

- At first you are generally in the dark; less than 5 percent of disgruntled people will express their feelings directly to you.
- However, the disgruntled people are not shy. The typical dissatisfied customer will share his or her feelings with perhaps 8 to 10 other people.
- As the "dissatisfaction virus" begins to spread, each of those 8 to 10 people passes the message along to perhaps another 20 people.
- Now, you are no longer in the dark; in fact, you are in a heightened state of damage control.

Unfortunately, it requires more than a dozen positive service experiences to overcome the impressions left by one negative incident. At that rate, you may never be able to restore your name to good health. So it is critical that this dissatisfaction virus not be allowed to incubate and spread. What means do you have to control it?

We advise that you begin by looking at the people you bring into your organization. As part of the hiring process, understand potential employees' beliefs and attitudes about customers and service. HReasy surveyed 1,000 applicants for customer service associate jobs, and to our dismay, they found the following:

- 41 percent of applicants disagreed with the statement "The customer is always right."
- 25 percent of applicants said it is virtually impossible to maintain a positive attitude when dealing with customers.
- 20 percent of applicants believed customers to be too demanding.
- 15 percent of applicants claimed that dealing with customers got in the way of the work they had to do.[2]

---

2 Source: http://findarticles.com/p/articles/mi_m3092/is_1998_Nov_23/ai_53347519.

What are your chances for creating a great service environment when hiring from that pool of applicants? Not very good, I'm afraid. Later in this book, we will discuss and counsel you on how to adopt a "hiring for attitude, training for skill" approach to staffing.

We now ask you to consider your own team or company and honestly assess your answers to the following questions:

- Are you encouraging or enabling an environment of discontent to fester and grow within your company or team?
- Are you losing clients for service-related reasons?
- Are your competitors creating more excitement and interest among their clients or, worse, among yours?
- Is your previously strong market share eroding or in a free fall?

If your answer is yes to even one of these questions, you must, without delay, undertake a change in your behaviors and approaches.

So Why Change?

The following are deemed Service Excellence companies, and they are regarded as some of America's most successful organizations:

Southwest Airlines
Apple
Marriott
Starbucks
Four Seasons Hotels
Whole Foods
FedEx Kinko's
Nordstrom
The Container Store
Target

The impetus for change is your desire to share in the traits that have become hallmarks of these Service Excellence companies:

- They are very profitable.
- They are consistently listed among *Fortune* magazine's "America's Most Admired Corporations."
- They have been listed among *Fortune* magazine's "Best Companies to Work for in America."
- They are brands that deliver a similar customer experience wherever you go.
- *How* they do *what* they do is a priority.
- Service Excellence is their bridge to customer loyalty.

Throughout this book we will cite examples drawn from these organizations, many with whom you are likely to interact on a frequent basis. Our purpose in benchmarking these companies is twofold:

1. To establish a personal association with Service Excellence behaviors, drawn from your own experience.
2. To reinforce the positive impact of Service Excellence behaviors when they extend to everyone, everywhere, every time.

As we go about our daily business, we are constantly managing crises that may stem from *what* you do. When your products or services fail or fall short of expectations, what happens? If your relationship with a client has no grounding in Service Excellence, you will likely find yourself in a tenuous situation. Conversely, if you have built your client relationship on a foundation of Service Excellence, you will probably "survive to serve another day." Service Excellence will be your safety net.

AN EARLY LEARNING

As a young boy growing up in Maspeth, Queens, I was always captivated by the circus. When Ringling Bros. came to New York City, I was one of the first in line to catch their opening show. As a circus fan, *all* of the acts excited me. However, I found the most impressive performers to be the tightrope walkers. I would marvel at their concentration and focus, their courage and skill, their grace and style, and their unblemished record of "never-fall" performances.

When the performers, resplendent in their costume attire, entered one of the three rings, they would focus on the wire some 100 feet in the air, visualizing "their walk." They would inspect the apparatus, making certain all the rigging was perfect. They would climb the rope ladder at one end of the rig and gingerly make their way onto one of the two platforms positioned at each end of the wire. They would gracefully remove their beautiful capes and rub resin onto their hands and the balancing pole.

Then the walk would begin. They would stare down at the wire and, carefully placing one foot in front of the other, ease their way onto the wire connecting the other platform some 50 feet away. At every performance, the tightrope walkers would reach the halfway point, and then appear to slip, stumble, or lose their footing. Amid audience gasps, they would struggle to right themselves and continue on to the other platform.

As I watched the acts rotate from ring to ring in Madison Square Garden, I saw performers check the security of their safety net before they "took to the wire." In my young mind, that diligent examination of the safety equipment magnified the daring of the act they were about to perform.

Never in all the performances I attended throughout my childhood (there had to be 20 or 25, I suppose) did a tightrope walker fall. "Why, then, did the tightrope walkers need a safety net?" I wondered. Their performances were always so perfect. Why did they bother to go through the time and trouble of setting up a safety net? They were so talented in *what* they did.

Years later, my childhood preoccupation with circus tightrope walkers served as a metaphor for the role of service in the context of client relationships. The tightrope walkers, with all their great skill and talent, performed *what* they did flawlessly. But in the event they were to fail, their safety net protected them from harm. In the rare instance that something bad happened, they would fall into the security of a net, bounce from it, and live to do another performance.

LESSON TO REMEMBER

What you do (your job) is clearly a challenging facet of the client or customer relationship. Despite the quality of your product and the manner in which it performs, some aspect of what you do is bound to fail at one time or another. If you do not have a "safety net" in place, your client relationships can be severely compromised or, worse, irreparably damaged.

Southwest Airlines lived this in March 2008, when it was uncovered that they failed to comply with FAA-mandated structural inspections of some of their planes. Clearly "what they do" had broken down. Service Excellence (*how* you do *what* you do) can be your safety net. Hopefully it was theirs.

In most cases, once you have logged months and years of Service Excellence, the inevitable slip will not hurt you.

2

Why Change?

Andrew Cuomo, the Attorney General of New York State, is . . . taking on the big and powerful. One of his first targets—Dell. Cuomo has filed suit against Dell, Inc., as a result of consumer complaints over alleged deceptive practices. The suit regards language around financing terms and interest rates that Cuomo says were used to lure in unwitting purchasers. Cuomo is seeking an injunction against the practices and as-yet unspecified damages for affected customers.

The suit also goes after Dell for poor customer service. It claims that Dell promised an "award-winning service" available "24 hours a day, seven days a week." Instead, the suit says that customers faced "nightmarish obstacles" to get any sort of technical or customer service. According to Cuomo, New York has received 700 complaints about Dell.[1]

It will be interesting to watch the outcome of this situation.

---

1 Source: www.switched.com/2007/05/16/new-york-attorney-general-sues-dell.

Why Should You Play a Role in the Increasing Erosion of Customer Service When There Are Alternatives?

This book will go on to reveal our proven approach for creating and sustaining a culture of Service Excellence. But before you embark on an exploration of this method, you must assert your willingness to change.

In a service culture, your attention will shift from a singular focus on the work you perform for clients (*what* you do) to the broader focus of *how* you perform the work on their behalf. Service Excellence creates the differentiation that gives rise to client loyalty, retention, and, ultimately, competitive advantage—the paramount outcome of a well-formed service relationship. As a means to achieve this end, we will encourage and support your change through our presentation of the following:

- A cultural transformation plan
- A Service Excellence strategy roadmap
- A companywide service initiative
- A means to competitive advantage through Service Excellence
- A profile of exceptional companies who practice Service Excellence

At the outset, note that Service Excellence cannot be exclusive to your external customers; the service practices you embrace with external clients must apply equally to your internal colleagues. Your company's ultimate success as a service-centric organization will be determined not only by how you treat those outside your organization but also by how well you serve one another internally. It stands to reason that companies who do not practice internal Service Excellence are highly unlikely to practice external Service Excellence. We will help you to identify the various roles people play that enable the successful achievement of your tasks and goals. These are the people you serve, and they should rightly be your focus whether inside or outside the company. Change is required internally as well as externally.

This is a how-to book that details a specific approach for achieving Service Excellence. It is about rudimentary client service standards, but more than that, it is about ensuring that your interactions with clients fulfill their expectations, resulting in loyal and enduring relationships. This noble goal is also fiscally responsible, as quantified by Robert Desatnick in his book *Managing to Keep Customers*: "The cost of landing a new customer is more than five times the cost of retaining an existing one."

We need not reflect further on the differences between good and bad service and the consequences of both. You experience those differences in every walk of your personal and professional lives. Your familiarities with the pleasure of good service and the pain of bad service are certainly distinct and instructive.

With your personal experiences as a benchmark, why wouldn't you make the conscious decision to transform? We challenge you, the reader, to continue reading and accept the challenge to change *how* you serve your clients and customers. As we proceed through this book, you must agree to be receptive and motivated to change. Our job will be to show you how to transform and make it last. The roadmap we present, if followed completely, achieves that. *That is our promise to you.*

So let's ponder the question more deeply: why change? Well, ultimately to develop competitive differentiation and attain success. Refer once again to the list of some of America's benchmark service companies cited in the previous chapter; their successes are good reasons why you should change. These companies enjoy continued success in large measure by providing Service Excellence to their clients and customers.

Change and Become a First Adopter

Many successful companies have defined service as a core com-
petency and have used it to build a bridge to competitive differentiation. They place their customers first, coach every associate
in the nuances of their service culture, monitor performance and
reward those who serve well, and strive unendingly for service
improvement. We would like to focus on three companies who
were first adopters of Service Excellence in their competitive set
and recognize the esteem afforded them by those they serve:

- *The Ritz-Carlton consistently ranks at or near the top in guest
  satisfaction among luxury hotels in the J.D. Power and Associates' annual North America Hotel Guest Satisfaction Index
  Studies.* The Ritz-Carlton has enjoyed leadership in the
  luxury category of service from the time that J.D. Power
  first began measuring guest satisfaction within this class of
  hotel. Their reputation and exemplary service have been
  chronicled and experienced by many. They have even
  teamed with New York University to teach their legendary
  approach to service to business people from around
  the world.
- *eBay is one of the most trusted companies in the United States
  for customer privacy, according to a 2004 Ponemon Institute
  survey.* eBay is a major player in the Internet marketplace,
  which, in its formative years, wrestled with consumer
  concerns about credit card fraud and identity theft. eBay
  addressed those fears by developing security and protection
  protocols that have transformed the way in which business
  is conducted on the Internet. They have since become one
  of the largest and fastest-growing companies in America.
- *Saturns are consistently among the top-ranked value-priced cars
  in J.D. Power and Associates' Customer Service Index Studies
  for the car industry.* Saturn differentiated itself by alleviat-

ing the anxiety associated with the new car negotiation and purchase experience. By adopting a "one-price" policy, with reasonable and fair price points, they redirected the conversation to one of service. Saturn is known for offering value-priced vehicles that are serviced by caring dealers with whom people have formed lasting relationships. In January 2007, at the North American International Auto Show, the Saturn AURA was named the "North American Car of the Year" by a jury of 49 automotive journalists from the United States and Canada.

Each of these companies was the first in their respective industries to identify service as a competitive field of play, to set their corporate direction accordingly, and to differentiate themselves from their competition by being the first to adopt a Service Excellence culture. As service pioneers in their fields, each company was also able to define the benchmarks against which service would be judged, further augmenting their competitive edge. Those who are the first to embrace change by *how* they do business are the ones who will achieve a competitive advantage in their fields—and it's always preferable to be the first to the game, make the rules, and bring your own ball.

• FedEx Kinko's •

A legendary example of the first-adopter theory can be found in the package delivery business. Fred Smith formed FedEx in 1971 out of his frustration with the service he received when mailing packages. He deemed the time to deliver, lack of reliability, and methods used for shipping unacceptable. He also realized that the business environment was changing such that fast and assured delivery of packages was increasingly becoming an absolute requirement for businesses of all sizes.

FedEx was the first company in the package delivery industry to create a business plan based on understanding current customers' needs, envisioning future needs, and developing an approach to satisfy both sets of needs by reliably delivering packages to customers the very next day.

As a result of creating a business based on anticipating and forecasting future needs of customers, FedEx enjoyed years of competitive advantage. They changed the industry and defined the service benchmarks, and their competitors had no choice but to follow.

The FedEx example illustrates an important approach to serving customers that will be the focus of Chapter 6 on understanding client needs. However, the concept is integral to achieving Service Excellence, so we will introduce it here as part of the rationale for deciding to change.

In my opinion, FedEx built their business strategy on the premise that every customer has two disparate sets of needs. The company understood that, first, people need their mail, packages, and products to reach their destinations swiftly. In the FedEx operating model of overnight delivery, satisfying that need was, and is, a hallmark of their business. It is a need that is satisfied by *what* they do. We call this satisfying a *hard need*.

However, FedEx also understood that many people had a second need that was possibly even more significant. This was a need to feel confident, certain, and assured that packages would be delivered within the agreed-upon time frame. This need for worry-free delivery, which is really an emotional need, is satisfied by *how* they do what they do. We call this satisfying a *soft need*.

We believe that just about every relationship with those you serve is based on these two sets of needs: hard needs, which are satisfied by *what* you do, and soft needs, those intangible, emotion-based needs, which are satisfied by *how* you do what you do. When you can discern and be sensitive to soft needs, you become capable of taking your customer relationships to a higher plane.

Once again:

- *A hard need is satisfied by what you do.* For example, "FedEx will deliver your package by 10:00 tomorrow morning."
- *A soft need is satisfied by how you do what you do.* For example, "FedEx makes you feel certain that your package will arrive the next day, enabling you to be worry free once it's in their hands."

FedEx is an ideal example of a company who understands both the hard needs and soft needs of their customers, and they are adept at satisfying both, resulting in the establishment of loyal and enduring relationships. And remember, in a competitive industry, those who are first to embrace change and focus on *how* they do business are the ones who will achieve competitive advantage.

Understanding and accepting these two disparate forms of needs is the foundation upon which your ability to change will be built.

FedEx was a first adopter, in that they originated the concept of delivering packages by 10 a.m. the following day. As a result, they changed the industry and forced their competitors to follow. However, they still enjoyed years of competitive advantage: they continue to set new service-level benchmarks, redefine the industry's field of play, and keep their competitors alert. Look what FedEx Kinko's does now: make it, print it, pack it, and ship it—globally! This ability to change in the direction of your customers' evolving needs results in category leadership and steadfast loyalty.

So How Difficult Is It to Change?

We believe that change can come about easily if you, as an individual or as a member of a team or company, are willing to embrace basic guidelines:

- Accept the need to change.
- Use common sense.
- Do what is right.
- Show concern for others.
- Be aware of what is happening around you.
- Learn to listen and to hear (they are different!).
- Be sensitive to others' needs.
- Put the other person in the relationship first.
- Commit to becoming purpose driven and values based.

If you are capable of doing the above and are willing to shift your focus to an individual or organizational behavior that is a service model designed to produce Service Excellence, then you are capable of change. The question you need to answer is, *will you change?*

Change, and You Will Differentiate Your Business from Your Competition

Fundamentally, there are just a few ways in which you can differentiate yourself from your competitors:

1. *Low price* is one differentiation strategy, but it can be problematic to maintain since it is easy for competitors to employ "beat-or-match" pricing tactics.
2. *Capital investments and innovation* that improve what you do (your product) provide differentiation until such time as those refinements are imitated or duplicated, at which point your differentiation is lost.
3. *Achieving Service Excellence* is the alternate, and less easily duplicated, method to achieving competitive differentiation.

This third approach, though simple in suggestion, takes patience and unwavering commitment to accomplish. Patience over a long period of time, supported by a strong transformation plan, is an absolute requirement for success. However, once this form of differentiation is achieved, it is very difficult for competitors to duplicate or counter. Service differentiation can endure, and, as a result, it can become a permanent bridge to loyalty.

So Why Is Service Excellence the Answer?

In the end, differentiation is what competition is all about. Service Excellence can be your competitive advantage. So why aren't more companies considering service as a strategy to create that differentiation? Perhaps companies do not appreciate the importance of Service Excellence or simply do not give service a high enough priority. Remember this compelling statistic:

> *According to the U.S. government, 78 percent of this country's gross domestic product is service based.*

The U.S. economy is no longer dominated by manufacturing, although even that sector interacts with internal and external customers that require services. So why is it so difficult for any company to decide to transform into an organization built upon the awareness of how a service strategy drives success? For those who choose to embrace this change, the question becomes, how do you go about creating the lasting relationships you seek based upon how you serve? This book provides the answer.

The challenge individuals and organizations face today is that, despite enhancing their product offerings with slick technology and creative positioning, they still struggle to differentiate themselves from their competitors. The encouraging news is that there are successful companies who have been achieving differentiation and competitive advantage through the Service Excellence they provide. Throughout this book we will convey to you examples of these notable success stories.

So Yet Again, Why Change?

This crisis in service that we all experience in every aspect of our lives is crying out for a solution. The solution resides in your recognition that, in order to compete more effectively in your workplace and the marketplace, you must transform *how* you do what you do. You must redirect your individual and organizational focus on your relationships with your clients. And you must understand how the extent of the loyalty given you by your individual clients is directly proportionate to your behavior toward them.

A POWERFUL LEARNING

In the autumn of 2005, I was reminded of a great lesson I had learned many years earlier from Irene DeGenarro, my wonderful assistant at Unilever. How she did what she did was remarkable.

It was November 8. I had been traveling with my son Rob and CROSSMARK's then COO Jim Borders, together with a video crew, to conduct full-day awareness meetings in support of the CROSSMARK transformation. Fortunately that week, because of a really tight schedule and their desire to videotape the sessions, we had the use of their company plane. As we were preparing for takeoff from the Bentonville, Arkansas, airport, I said to Rob, "I can't see well out of my left eye!" Not knowing the cause or understanding the severity, we decided to carry on with our itinerary and fly to Birmingham. Upon arrival we went to the University of Alabama hospital, known for their eye specialty, which is where I received the diagnosis that I'd had a small stroke, and that the resultant sight loss would be permanent.

Despite this upsetting news, I was determined to uphold my obligation to CROSSMARK and facilitate the planned session we had scheduled for their Birmingham associates the next day. Rob and Jim reluctantly agreed to abide by my wishes, but they drew the line at allowing me to continue on to Charlotte for our subsequent group session. Instead, they insisted that I return to Los Angeles to confer with my own doctors about why I'd had this stroke and how to prevent another such occurrence.

Over the next two and a half weeks, I underwent numerous tests and had medical consultations with five highly respected specialists from Los Angeles to New York to Phoenix. As luck would have it, the diagnostic tests were inconclusive, and the physicians held conflicting opinions about what constituted appropriate treatment. Three of the doctors concluded that surgery was potentially too dangerous to perform, and two deemed that surgery was medically indicated in order to pinpoint the source of my stroke and prevent a recurrence. So I was faced with a very difficult personal decision. I didn't know which course of action was the right one, although the majority opinion certainly did not support surgery. All I knew was that my primary goal was to do everything possible to ensure the best outcome for my future.

It was the day before Thanksgiving, and I was struggling with the decision now in front of me. That evening I went out to dinner, and upon opening my wallet to pay the bill, I discovered a small slip of paper that Irene, my assistant, had given me 13 years earlier. At that time, I was in the hospital faced with a similar decision about my health. Irene had come to visit, and when she said her good-byes, she handed me this slip of paper and said, "Read this; it may help." On it, Irene had typewritten a quote from James A. Baldwin that ultimately had a large impact on my decision:

> Not everything that is faced can be changed, but nothing can
> be changed until it is faced.

On the way home from dinner that Thanksgiving eve, inspired by Irene, I came to a decision about my treatment plan. I chose to face my condition head on and, despite the risk, elect for surgery as recommended by two of the five physicians. I immediately called my cardiologist, Neil Buchbinder, and my surgeon, David Cossman, who scheduled surgery for the day after Thanksgiving. I was not certain about the impact surgery would have on my future health, but if these two dissenting physicians were correct in their diagnoses, I knew it could change for the better.

The minority opinion turned out to be correct. When surgery was performed that Friday at Cedars-Sinai, the doctors were able to establish conclusively that my stroke had been caused by plaque breaking away from a wall in the carotid artery on the left side of my neck. Furthermore, they discovered another mound of plaque that was primed to break away, which would have undoubtedly triggered additional acute health problems. The surgery did succeed in ensuring the best outcome for my future, even beyond my expectations and those of my doctors.

LESSON TO REMEMBER

Deciding to make a change can be difficult and uncomfortable. When the decision to change is of particular importance, a bit of study, research, and dialogue is required. However, if deep down you believe changing is the right thing to do, you must make the decision to move forward. Perhaps something great will happen; perhaps nothing different will occur. That is the chance you take. But if you do not face the fact that change is required and act upon it, you can be assured that nothing will improve.

How **you do** *what* **you do will determine who you will become.**

—Bob Livingston

3

How to Change: The Roadmap

It all begins, continues, and ends with clients. We stopped saying "customers" and started saying "clients." Semantics? Maybe, but to us "customer" sounded too transitory. A "customer" completes a transaction with a business and then leaves. We don't want anyone to leave. A "client" on the other hand, establishes a long-lasting relationship with a business that includes the familiarity of a common history and the interdependence of a joined future.

—Jeff Weitzen, former president and COO, Gateway

In the context of *how* we do *what* we do, we agree with this distinction between *clients* and *customers*; furthermore, we believe that everyone you serve is a client regardless of whether he or she is internal or external to your organization. As you continue through this book, we will assume you have accepted our challenge to change the way in which you serve your clients. The balance of this book will be relevant if you, as an individual, are willing to commit to a personal transformation of *how* you do *what* you do.

The transformation of a company's culture to one that is defined by Service Excellence requires universal associate engagement. This service strategy transformation begins at the top, with the commitment to a companywide culture change from the most senior level of an organization (for example, the board of directors). For it to succeed, a compelling message that describes how the total organization will be called upon to support, guide, and ensure the longevity of this cultural transformation must be an integral part of the process.

This chapter discusses how to embark on your cultural transformation to Service Excellence. Adopting a service strategy as your company's means to attaining a competitive advantage will, in time, prove to be a revolutionary decision. However, it is not an effortless undertaking. It requires the full support and ardent endorsement of senior management, a commitment to permanence through the ongoing cultivation of Service Excellence, the full involvement of *all* operating disciplines within the company, and the complete engagement and participation by every last associate, regardless of his or her role in the organization.

In order to succeed, certain concessions are required. Every person in your company must embrace the commitment to Service Excellence and actively participate in the process described in this book. People must change their attitudes about clients and modify their behavior in client relationships. Most important, extraordinary patience is required throughout the entire process. It requires a significant investment of time, so patience is needed with the learning curve, the company, yourself, and, most important, one another. It is our belief that your patience and tolerance for change will grow as your service culture takes root and you achieve the success that stems from competitive differentiation.

How to Approach Transforming Yourself or a Company

You must first accept that transforming yourself or a company requires a significant investment of time. Changing a culture requires a great deal of planning, meetings, and ongoing coaching. The nature of internal and external client dialogue must change, which will necessitate new listening and feedback skills that must be taught and practiced. New behaviors and attitudes, which are essential to any successful transformation, must become ingrained in the culture, which also takes time. A cultural transformation requires very little in the way of capital investment but a great deal in the way of time, across all levels of the company and particularly in the early stages.

To initiate a change of this nature and magnitude, each employee must first recognize that "service" permeates every internal and external process and relationship. From there, it is critical that all associates become *passionate* about serving their clients and colleagues consistently well. This requires a comprehension of the "soft needs"—an understanding that *how* associates perform their work is just as important as the work they perform. In most instances this will represent a major shift from how employees are currently recognized and rewarded.

The prospect of getting everyone on board is daunting, particularly when you consider how badly so many organizations treat their employees today. Consider the results of our very unscientific investigation in which we searched the term *employee dissatisfaction* on Google and received close to 2 million hits in 0.14 seconds! It is not difficult to see that poor treatment of employees has reached epidemic proportions in today's workplace.

A differing, and significantly more uplifting, perspective is presented by *Fortune* magazine's annual Best Companies to Work For survey. In January 2007, they reported the 10 best companies in the United States to be these:

1. Google
2. Genentech
3. Wegmans Food Markets
4. The Container Store
5. Whole Foods Markets
6. Network Appliance
7. S. C. Johnson & Son

8. The Boston Consulting Group
9. Methodist Hospital System
10. W. L. Gore & Associates

In 2007, 446 private and public companies vied for the top.
And 100,000 workers evaluated their employers, making this
by far the largest simultaneous employee survey in corporate
America. That's one thing that hasn't—and won't—change
about the list: Employees decide who gets a spot.

—Robert Levering and Michael Moskowitz, "In Good
Company," *Fortune* magazine, January 29, 2007

This annual survey, now in its tenth year, is the best source we
have found for uncovering how people feel about the companies
for whom they work. Companies are rated highly by their associates for varying reasons; but regardless of why people feel good
about their employers, the important point is that they do. And
when people feel positively about their work environment, that
attitude pervades all of their interactions with others.

The service process that we will discuss in this book is based on
the commonsense approach of treating people the way *they* want to
be treated. Dr. Tony Alessandra has called this the "Platinum Rule":

> *Treat others the way they want to be treated. Ah hah! What
> a difference. The Platinum Rule accommodates the feelings
> of others. The focus of relationships shifts from "this is what
> I want, so I'll give everyone the same thing" to "let me first
> understand what they want and then I'll give it to them."*

How Do You Begin to Instill the Service Spirit?

A cultural transformation must begin with the senior levels of
your organization where a series of beliefs, or values, can be de-

fined to be your guide as you embark upon changing how you do what you do.

In the introduction, we indicated we would use CROSSMARK, the sales and marketing agency with whom we worked closely for about four years, to illustrate a successful real-life cultural transformation. We believe this to be a compelling endorsement of implementing a service culture because CROSSMARK's new culture continues to succeed and to thrive, and during our development of that culture, fervent supporters emerged throughout the course of the process.

• The CROSSMARK Story •

In 2003, CROSSMARK's Executive Management Committee came to a unanimous decision to champion a cultural transformation of their company. As solid evidence of their commitment, they named Jim Borders, then COO, to be the steward of the day-to-day operations required for a successful transformation. It was Jim who challenged me and Rob to design an approach for building awareness throughout their entire organization of the changes CROSSMARK sought to achieve.

We began by holding a series of meetings with CROSSMARK's training and human resources departments to clarify our role in this process and gain their support. At first we sensed a hesitancy to "turn over to us" an endeavor they deemed to be their responsibility. This was but one of the many times that Jim's involvement proved invaluable. He was able to assure his organization that we were there only to facilitate the process of creating awareness; the true transformation would be realized ultimately through their internal leadership once the awareness and commitment had been broadly secured.

Working with Jim, we identified a core constituency of CROSSMARK associates who would become the focus of their organization's cultural transformation. In all, we identified 1,700 associates to engage. Having established this target audience, we developed plans for a series of five distinct meetings that would be conducted over a period of 30 months in 30 locations in North America. Attendance was mandatory at each of the five sessions, during which the entire day was devoted solely to the topic of transforming CROSSMARK's culture and achieving Service Excellence.

In conjunction with Jim, Rob created the presentation and support materials to ensure that they were specific to CROSSMARK and relevant to its business model. We keyed off many of the great service companies with whom their associates regularly interacted, using these examples of Service Excellence as a benchmark. Understanding how these successful organizations did what they did created a more thoughtful and personal awareness of the tangible aspects of Service Excellence for this core participant group.

Jim Borders' presence at each and every meeting was absolutely essential for our success, and it signaled to the participants that this was not just another "program of the month" from corporate headquarters. Jim opened and closed each session, and his remarks underscored the message that this important undertaking was ultimately designed to create a competitive advantage for CROSSMARK by differentiating *how* they did what they did from their competition.

So how successful were we in instilling a service spirit at CROSS-MARK? As you would imagine, we met with some initial skepticism and some resistance, and we observed many associates waiting to gauge the company's dedication prior to committing their time and energy. But the collaborative awareness sessions, unwavering support from senior management, and commitment of time and resources eventually reinforced the veracity of this program. Looking back on the four years this process took to complete and evaluating the feedback and results from those involved in the transformation, we felt certain that a majority of their associates believed in and welcomed CROSSMARK's desire to change.

In subsequent chapters we will present the details of this initial phase of CROSSMARK's cultural transformation. But first, it is important to discuss other decisions that must be made prior to embarking on this process.

How Do You Create a Core Ideology That Is Service Based?

This is a very thought provoking question, but it had to be resolved at the beginning of the process of creating an awareness of Service Excellence among CROSSMARK's associates. More specifically, how does a cultural transformation of this nature impact the following areas:

- Performance evaluations
- Recruiting and hiring
- Training
- Motivation and rewards
- Internal needs assessments
- Cultural development
- Client feedback

CROSSMARK formed the Service Champions Committee after the first phase of the process was concluded, and the company entrusted them with the responsibility for resolving these matters. This committee was composed of individuals who had distinguished themselves as "thought leaders" capable of shaping, guiding, and monitoring the progress of cultural transformation. Eventually, the committee evolved and became the ongoing advisory and planning body for Service Excellence transformation, developing plans for creating and sustaining CROSSMARK's new core ideology. Initially, however, this group was asked to accomplish the following:

- Recommend and develop hiring guidelines to ensure that a service orientation was inherent in all new employees.

- Revise performance review criteria to integrate service successes.
- Modify the bonus program to incorporate a Service Excellence component.
- Develop recognition programs to publicly reward great service providers.
- Amend the salary increase guidelines to factor in service performance.
- Conduct field surveys to establish baselines for client and employee attitudes.

In a cultural transformation of this nature, it is essential to convey the message that change is required of the entire organization—not just certain segments. It must be endorsed by the senior leadership, and it must be companywide in scope. It is a long-term commitment; it is not a contest, motivational tool, or performance measurement program. It is about serving customers better than anyone, both internally and externally, from which competitive advantage based on differentiation will emerge.

Ultimately, everyone must own and be guardians of the new culture. In that, you are all equals, as illuminated by the following fundamental principle:

> *Most companies have a hierarchy of responsibility that pertains to what you do within the company. This is necessary. However, in regard to how you do what you do within a company, there is no hierarchy. Everyone is equal in matters of service.*

A True Service Excellence Company Does Not Tolerate Double Standards

- Service Excellence cannot be limited to your external clients; the same principles must also apply to your coworkers.
- In fact, anyone who enables you to accomplish your tasks and goals is, by definition, a person you serve. Both in-

ternal colleagues and external clients qualify to be in this category.

- The extent to which your company succeeds in its endeavor to be service driven will be determined by how you treat those outside your organization, as well as how you serve one another internally.

The scope of a cultural transformation is so broad that you will likely need the support of study groups, grassroots initiatives, and internal disciples to achieve success. It is also vital that you not overlook the importance of "high touch" in shaping your new culture, as adroitly described by Procter & Gamble's A. G. Lafley in an article in the April/May 2006 issue of *Chief Executive* magazine regarding his selection as 2006 CEO of the Year:

> *He believes in the "high touch" to shape P&G's internal culture. "Let's face it—we're big," he says. "We have 135,000 employees with Gillette on the ground in 80 countries or so. Just communicating across time and space, coordinating across time and space, is very difficult. We use the Intranet. We're all running around with BlackBerries and cell phones. But we also try to use a lot of high touch [personal engagement].*
>
> *"You have to bring people together to learn from each other," he explains. "Getting employees to engage with each other in these ways seems to help them concentrate on the human dimension of understanding consumers." P&G had "gotten into bad habits," he says. "We were spending too much time in meetings. We were spending too much time with our head in our computer. We were spending too much time sending e-mail to each other."*

The Roadmap to Service Excellence

To get somewhere, you need to start somewhere. Our roadmap does just that: It lays out the route to follow in order to get to Service

Excellence. It is an approach we developed that guides you through the process of creating your strategy to transform your culture.

An initiative as important as this requires you to construct a comprehensive plan, or roadmap, that is specific, flows logically, and is continuously aligned from beginning to end. The roadmap we developed consists of *five steps* that can be followed by an individual, team, or organization in proactively managing relationships with clients and colleagues:

1. Develop your Purpose.
2. Establish your Values.
3. Understand client needs.
4. Satisfy those needs.
5. Create Service Action Plans.

Purpose and Values (steps 1 and 2) go hand-in-hand; your Purpose defines *who* you want to be, while your Values *guide* you toward becoming that which you desire to be. In subsequent chapters we discuss Purpose and Values independently, so as to enable a thorough examination of each of these interrelated steps. For both to have meaning, you must define them for yourself if they are to become central to your identity. Assuming someone else's Purpose and Values will create internal conflict if they are incompatible with your own character.

In our discussion of the third step, understand client needs, we probe the differences between hard needs and soft needs. This distinction is fundamental to our approach to Service Excellence; so a solid grasp of hard versus soft needs, and the acknowledgment of their basic differences, will be your catalyst for transformation. Only when you truly understand and live this concept will you be able to succeed in serving clients and colleagues.

Satisfying client needs, the fourth step, truly brings to life the concept of *how* you do *what* you do. We introduce the idea of "putting the other person first" as an essential element of Service Excellence. We discuss ways in which you can create memorable experiences for your clients by exceeding their expectations and utilizing your imagination to bring them fresh and creative ideas. We focus on the art of personal interaction, talk about customizing behaviors to situations, and stress the vital role that listening and communicating play in satisfying client needs.

Creating Service Action Plans is the fifth and final step of the roadmap. These written action plans guide your behaviors and define the framework for how to operate successfully in your service relationships. A Service Action Plan is created for everyone you have identified as someone you serve—clients, customers, and colleagues. Based on the frequency of contact, Service Action Plans are created for individuals or constituencies. Service Action Plans must be continuously monitored and updated based on your knowledge of changing client and marketplace needs and their impact on service requirements. This step is critical to the successful implementation of any cultural service transformation.

Your roadmap to Service Excellence must be comprehensive, have a logical flow, and be continuously aligned from beginning to end. Complementing these steps are other factors essential for success including service-oriented personal traits, a drive for continuous improvement, a commitment to grow and nurture the new culture, and clear ownership of the process. These facets of the total process are discussed in future chapters. Although it may sound complex, once you begin your journey to Service Excellence, you will find the five steps to be a simple and straightforward guide to achieving your goal.

AN IMPORTANT LEARNING

Do you recall a single person or event that made a dramatic impact on your career by guiding you to change? One such instance has stayed with me throughout my life.

My first job was a territory representative with the Campbell Soup Company, and I was struggling with many aspects of the role. I had convinced myself that sales and service work was just not for me, and I had decided to resign before becoming too entrenched. So one day I left my territory early, and I drove home to sort out my company supplies in order to relinquish them when I resigned the following day. When I arrived, my mother was surprised to see me and asked why I was home from work so early.

I said, "I'm having a very bad time, Mom. I'm just not cut out for selling. I can't seem to make many sales, regardless of how hard I try. So I'm going to put my things in order and resign tomorrow." She looked at me with great concern and calmly said, "Let's talk about it over a cup of tea."

Before the water had even come to a boil, my mother asked, "What's wrong, Bob? This doesn't sound like you." I explained that I was very discouraged by the constant rejection from customers and my seeming inability to convince them to try new ideas. I felt that all of my hard work didn't yield any results, so the only responsible thing to do was to leave before I became too committed to the job.

She did not respond, and we finished our tea in nerve-racking silence.

As my mother was clearing the table, she turned back to me and quietly said, "Why don't you go to your room, work a bit harder, and perhaps try a different approach?" So I left the kitchen, went to my room, and did exactly that. I began to work harder and differently. I organized my fact books and presentation case; I brushed up on my product knowledge and studied my product plans; I memorized price lists and studied my merchandising proposals.

I spent the remainder of the afternoon and all evening working hard, feeling differently, but not yet able to fully understand the change that was coming over me. I felt as though I'd uncovered a new approach, or roadmap, to how I did what I did. I had been ready to take the easy way out by quitting rather than trying to meet the challenge by exploring the possibilities of change.

At ten o'clock that evening, my mother and father came in to say good-night. "Are you almost done? It's getting late, and you have a big day tomorrow. How is your work? Did you do well?" I told them that I was nearly finished, and they simply said "Good" and closed my door. That was the extent of our conversation. I continued working for another two hours, and then I packed my materials—not to resign but to go to work the next day.

I arrived at 7:30 the next morning, well before the store had even opened. I felt energized by the work I had done the prior day, and I was excited as I carried my heavy sales bag into my first call. That call was successful, as were many subsequent calls that day, culminating in the most successful day I'd had to date in this, my first job out of college. As the day drew to a close and I was driving home, I experienced the real exhilaration that comes from successfully serving clients. It was the beginning of the most rewarding and enjoyable career I could have ever hoped for.

That day I learned an amazing lesson from my mom, a person for whom I had tremendous admiration. Over that cup of tea, her simple but firm suggestion that I work harder and take a new approach taught me how to create a new roadmap for myself and my career. How ironic that, after my first job with the Campbell Soup Company, I went on to a very successful 30-year career with the Lipton Tea Company. Thank you, Mom and Dad!

LESSON TO REMEMBER

At certain times it becomes imperative that we discover a new approach in our professional lives—a new roadmap will take us in a direction that, for whatever reason, we never before considered.

It is our hope that this book will be your catalyst to change. We will show you how to change, and we'll provide the roadmap.

2

The Transformation

4

Develop Your Purpose

About Purpose

What is the purpose of a Purpose? Purpose defines you. It is *why* you do what you do. It drives *how* you do what you do. It is how you want to be remembered and why. The one true measure of performance for a service-centric individual, team, or company is the extent to which reality (goal achievement) converges with client perceptions. To be successful, you must first determine what it is that you wish to be successful doing and then determine how you will achieve that. You must envision the end before you begin. Purposeful people and organizations establish expectations internally and externally so that their constituents clearly understand the look and feel of the desired end result. In the words of the renowned Hall of Fame philosopher Yogi Berra, "If you don't know where you're going, you're liable to end up somewhere else!"

Since Purpose defines you, a self-serving Purpose will communicate to others that your actions are solely for your own benefit. Conversely, a client-centric Purpose will convey an inherent focus on the welfare of your clients. It is essential to the success of your cultural transformation to create an environment in which your associates believe in and foster the power of a client-centric

Purpose. Successful organizations continually seek success. They also recognize that success, individually and collectively, can be achieved only in partnership with their clients and one another.

What Is the Difference between a Purpose and a Mission?

Before we begin developing our Purpose, we would like to clarify the difference between a Purpose and a Mission. Businesses tend to use *Mission* and *Purpose* interchangeably, but these terms mean different things, and understanding the distinction between them will serve you well as you work on defining your Purpose.

According to *Webster's Third New International Dictionary*, a *Mission* is "a task with which one is charged, a continuing task or responsibility that one is destined or fitted to do or specially called upon to undertake." In the context of achieving Service Excellence, your Mission describes *what* you do.

The same source defines *Purpose* as "something that someone sets out before himself as an objective to be attained: an end to be kept in view." Again, in the context of achieving Service Excellence, your Purpose describes *how* you do what you do.

To illustrate this fine distinction between a Purpose and a Mission, we refer once again to some of our benchmark service companies.

What Is Their Business?

Let us begin by defining the "business" of these companies, which will help us later to distinguish between their Mission and their Purpose. Some of the following descriptions are as the companies see themselves, while others are as we, the client, see them.

• Starbucks •

We are not in the coffee business serving people. We are in
the people business serving coffee.

—Howard Schultz, Starbucks founder

This declarative statement by Howard Schultz makes clear the
business of Starbucks. They are committed to offering the best of
coffees and, with hundreds of possible drink combinations, satisfying
a multitude of their customers' taste preferences. In so doing, they
create an environment that ensures that people will enjoy their Starbucks experience. That is their business, isn't it?

In the early stages of my career in New York City, I recall taking
coffee breaks at a corner restaurant or street vendor, sipping the
one variety of coffee served (black) from a small Styrofoam cup. Talk
about transformations. What was a routine and uninspired break
from one's workday has become a pleasurable experience, replete
with comfortable chairs, great music, and friendly "baristas."

• Southwest Airlines •

As a seasoned traveler, *my* opinion is that Southwest Airlines is in
the business of transporting customers to their U.S. destinations
safely, cost-effectively, and on time.

This exceptional company provides one of the most fascinating
illustrations of the concept that *how* you do *what* you do ultimately
defines who you become. In an industry characterized by escalating
and volatile costs, erratic fuel supplies, complex and contentious
labor entanglements, and the specter of terrorism, Southwest has
managed to grow into one of the safest, most economical, reliable
airlines flying today.

The Southwest story has been analyzed broadly in an attempt to re-
create their successful business model. It is truly admirable that, in

an industry as problematic as any we observe, they have remained profitable throughout their history, and they repeatedly appear on *Fortune*'s list of America's Most Admired Corporations.

• Marriott •

Marriott is in the business of providing their guests with accommodations around the world that satisfy a wide variety of tastes, geographic requirements, and financial considerations. With a diverse portfolio of brands, Marriott has the capacity to appeal to an extremely broad base of consumers.

In one of Bill Marriott, Jr.'s earliest blog entries (at 75 years old, he started "blogging"!), he described each of the brands in Marriott's portfolio. The Ritz-Carlton and JW Marriott hotels are their high-end brands, renowned for service and style. The Renaissance and Marriott Hotels & Resorts brands provide a full range of services for business travelers and vacationing families. Courtyard by Marriott was designed to fill a niche for business travelers who require full functionality with minimum frills. SpringHill Suites cater to "enjoyment seekers" who are looking to have fun while traveling on business. Fairfield Inns are designed for guests who want that perfect balance between price and quality. Residence Inns offer "extended-stay guests" a comfortable, residential environment, which is also true of TownePlace Suites but at an even more affordable price.

Marriott opened their 3,000th hotel in 2007, a testimony to the success they've achieved by executing a fairly complex strategy of "being all things to all people."

Contrast Mission and Purpose

So if you accept the premise that *Mission* defines *what* we do and *Purpose* defines *how* we do what we do, then *Purpose* really tells the world how we want to be remembered:

- *Starbucks' Mission* is this: "Establish Starbucks as the premier purveyor of the finest coffee in the world while maintaining our uncompromising principles as we grow and develop enthusiastically satisfied customers all of the time" *(what)*.

  Their *Purpose*, as described by Howard Schultz, states:

  > "We are not in the coffee business serving people. We are in the people business serving coffee. We continually are reminded of the powerful need and desire for human contact and for community, which is a new powerful force in determining consumer choices. The Starbucks environment has become as important as the coffee itself" *(how)*.
  > —Joseph Michelli, *The Starbucks Experience*

- *Southwest's Mission* might be described as transporting customers to their U.S. destinations safely, cost-effectively, and on time *(what)*.

  Their *Purpose* is "dedication to the highest quality of Customer Service delivered with a sense of warmth, friendliness, individual pride, and Company Spirit" *(how)*.

- *Marriott's Mission* could well be described as providing accommodations around the world through a diverse portfolio of brands that satisfies a wide variety of tastes, geographic requirements, and financial considerations *(what)*.

  Their *Purpose* is "to win in service by proactively offering customers the most valuable assistance, information, and support in a uniquely warm and caring manner" *(how)*.

As you can see, each company supports its Mission with a Purpose. By having a Purpose that creates Service Excellence, each of these companies has become a standout in its field.

Develop a Purpose

• CROSSMARK •

In the previous chapter we noted the importance of inviting those who will live the Purpose to create it. When the Purpose is crafted by people outside the organization or is handed down from above, it may be very difficult to live by.

In the first phase of CROSSMARK's cultural transformation process, we conducted 35 meetings around the country. One of the primary undertakings of each session was to have the attendees work on developing the Purpose. To the credit of CROSSMARK's senior executives, they supported the grassroots effort to create a recommendation for how the company Purpose should read. This portion of the meeting was highly interactive and animated, enabling associates from various work disciplines to collaborate on this important step of the process.

To begin, we divided the attendees into discussion groups of 8 to 10 people, and asked each group to discuss their opinions and reach consensus on the following questions:

- What is CROSSMARK's Purpose in serving clients?
- What is your role in serving clients?
- Whom do you serve?
- How do you want to be remembered?
- What are the behaviors that differentiate *what* you do for a client from *how* you do it?
- What is required to build loyalty?

We offered guidance on brainstorming techniques, which we'll explore in more detail in Chapter 9. At the conclusion of their idea generation exercise, the people at each table consolidated their thoughts into a short statement of Purpose. From that, the groups presented their recommended Purpose to the full audience who, by popular vote, selected the best statement from their meeting. From this consensus, each table reconvened to brainstorm ideas on how best to word the statement of Purpose.

At the conclusion of these meetings, we had a total of 35 statements of Purpose for submission to CROSSMARK's Steering Committee. After careful consideration, the committee selected the Purpose statement they felt best represented the people in their company. This final statement, from the St. Louis group, was not altered in any way—testimony to the fact that CROSSMARK acknowledged this chosen Purpose to be "the best of the best":

> CROSSMARK is dedicated to building and maintaining long-term partnerships with our clients, customers, and associates by providing an exceptional level of service delivered with passion, integrity, innovation, and consistency.

Everyone in the company was unusually excited and pleased with the final statement of Purpose. It was direct, decisive, and contained a stated outcome. It also had the added quality of articulating desired behaviors by declaring that CROSSMARK associates exhibit four significant traits in their relationships with clients and colleagues: *passion, integrity, innovation, and consistency*. Traits play an important role in satisfying client needs, so it was inspiring to see them integrated into the statement of Purpose.

We conclude our review of Purpose by applying the *what-how* distinction to CROSSMARK's Mission and Purpose:

> *Their Mission.* To be the best business services company within the consumer goods industry, delivering customized client solutions and unparalleled execution *(what)*.

> *Their Purpose.* CROSSMARK is dedicated to building and maintaining long-term partnerships with our clients, customers, and associates by providing an exceptional level of service delivered with passion, integrity, innovation, and consistency *(how)*.

Living Your Purpose

> Vision without action is merely a dream. Action without vision just passes the time. Vision with action can change the world.
>
> —Joel Barker, independent scholar and futurist

It is one thing to define your Purpose; it is another to actually live your Purpose. Living your Purpose means giving value to the words. Consider, once again, Southwest Airlines. Their Purpose is "to be dedicated to the highest quality of Customer Service delivered with a sense of warmth, friendliness, individual pride, and Company Spirit." How do they live their Purpose?

- Their Purpose is practiced consistently and by every person in the company.
- They position themselves as a customer service business that happens to provide air transportation.
- They tell their people to "do what it takes" to make the customer happy.
- They try never to inconvenience their customers.
- They always try to do the right thing.
- They instill confidence in their customers.

As a result of living their Purpose, these are some of Southwest Airlines' achievements:

- Voted most admired airline from 1997 to 2005, and No. 2 most admired company by *Fortune* magazine in March 2003
- Listed in the top 10 of *Fortune*'s most admired companies in each of the last nine years
- Earned $499 million in 2006—more than all other major airlines combined

- Recorded 34 uninterrupted years of profitability
- Acknowledged as the best-performing airline stock from 1972 to 2006
- Maintained a near-perfect safety record in 39 years of flying
- Grown to have more planes and carry more passengers than any other airline

For Purpose to have life and meaning, we ask you to recollect and commit to memory two important facets of our discussion:

1. Whether you are an individual or part of a team or a company, for Purpose to have meaning you must create it for yourself or have a hand in its creation.
2. Since Purpose is about *how* you do what you do, the statement of Purpose must translate into behaviors you are comfortable adopting.

In the case of CROSSMARK, their statement of Purpose was born out of a collaboration of 1,700 associates who felt an ownership of the end result. And, by specifying the traits required to fulfill their Purpose, the expected behaviors of this organization were evident. The very words suggest how CROSSMARK expects their associates to live the Purpose: Building and maintaining long-term partnerships will result from the following:

- Passion (behavior and attitude)
- Integrity (values)
- Innovation (imagination)
- Consistency (requirement)

Your Purpose, coupled with your behaviors for living that Purpose, can change your world.

A MEMORABLE LEARNING

In 1984, I was asked to attend a meeting at the Ritz-Carlton hotel in Laguna Niguel, California. I called ahead for reservations, and I was informed by the agent that this property was scheduled to open at the time of my arrival, so their service might not meet Ritz-Carlton standards. She was hopeful that I would still make reservations, but she felt obligated to inform me of the hotel's newness. I went ahead with my original plans, and upon arrival, I learned that the hotel had in fact been open less than a week.

As I pulled my rental car into the hotel's driveway, I was preoccupied with an important conference call that required my participation shortly after my arrival. I was greeted at my car by the doorman, who removed my luggage from the trunk and said, "Welcome to the Ritz-Carlton, Mr. Livingston. We've been expecting you. Please go to the front desk to register, and I'll send your bags right up to your room."

As I made my way to the front desk, I couldn't help but wonder how this doorman knew my name. Never before had I experienced this kind of name recognition when checking into a hotel. I registered and hurried to my room to join the conference call, but to my surprise and disappointment, I discovered that the telephone in my room was not working.

I left my room to find a house phone, and upon picking up the receiver, I was greeted by a telephone repairman who said, "I have a feeling you're Mr. Livingston, and you're calling to report that the phone in your room isn't working. I had informed the front desk that your phone was out of order, but with everyone so new, I guess they slipped up and assigned you that room by mistake. I'm on my way up to your room right now, and I will be bringing you the key to a new room where I know for certain the phone is working."

The telephone repairman arrived in a matter of minutes, escorted me to a new room with a working phone, and set me up to join my conference call on time. As the call began, I glanced over my shoulder and noticed that he'd also moved my luggage to the new room. He quietly whispered, "Here are your bags. I'll be certain that the front desk makes note of your room switch, so you won't be interrupted while on your call."

Despite my preoccupation with the conference call, I couldn't help but think about how impressed I was with how that individual did what he did. It surely wasn't his responsibility to bring me a new room key, escort me to my room, move my bags, or be certain the front desk had noted the room switch. But like all Ritz-Carlton associates, he cared and felt responsible for providing Service Excellence to all guests.

When I checked out of the hotel two days later, I asked the doorman how he had known my name when I arrived. "Oh, that's quite simple," he replied. "All I had to do was read the name on your luggage tags while removing the bags from your car."

Quite simple, perhaps, but isn't that the marvel of how we do what we do? By 1984, I had checked into nearly 800 hotels and not once, until that moment, had a doorman ever greeted me by name. In the years since, I cannot calculate the number of hotels I've checked into. But I can tell you that the number of times I've been greeted by name, in the fashion of that Ritz-Carlton doorman, totals perhaps a dozen. How very disappointing.

LESSON TO REMEMBER

Don't you have to wonder why, when many of the steps to Service Excellence are this simple, the state of service can't broadly improve? The answer is also quite simple. Service doesn't improve when people don't care enough to serve others well. That is the sad bottom line.

My experience at the Laguna Niguel Ritz-Carlton many years ago is emblematic of how they do what they do. From the reservations agent to the doorman to the telephone repairman, everyone understood the standard of service to which Ritz-Carlton's associates are expected to adhere. They all live their Purpose.

The Ritz-Carlton Hotel Credo (Mission and Purpose combined). The Ritz-Carlton is a place where the genuine care and comfort of our guests is our highest Mission (*what*). We pledge to provide the finest personal service and facilities for our guests who will always enjoy a warm, relaxed, yet refined ambience. The Ritz-Carlton experience enlivens the senses, instills well-being, and fulfills even the unexpressed wishes and needs of our guests (*how*).

5

Establish Your Values

In the past decade of intense competition and financial pressures from Wall Street, we need not recount the damage caused by the loss of Values inside American businesses. We watched in dismay the procession of companies who pushed their Values aside in the zealous pursuit of profits. Many of the principal offenders have been identified and held accountable for their actions. But central to these difficult situations was the absence of a meaningful set of Values by which everyone lived. We contend that the "rank and file" was, for the most part, purposeful in cause and Values based in behavior. However, it has become clear that many of the senior leadership had lost their way.

Purpose and Values go hand-in-hand. As we discussed in the previous chapter, your Purpose defines who you want to be. Your Values will guide you toward becoming that which you desire. Establishing your Values is the second step in the roadmap to achieving Service Excellence, but this step is inextricably linked to developing your Purpose.

Your Values, as with your Purpose, must be embraced by all. There can be no exceptions. As an individual undertaking this five-step process, you must personally determine your Values. If you are approaching this process as a team, you must gain consensus of team Values. As this chapter unfolds, we will discuss the creation of company Values during a companywide transformation to Service Excellence.

We begin by establishing common definitions for *Values* and *attitudes*, *behaviors*, and *motives* as they all impact Values:

Values.   Guidelines that control your behavior
Attitudes.   How you think
Behaviors.   How you act
Motives.   The reasons you do things

In this chapter, we will answer the questions: Who should establish Values? How should they be formed? How detailed need they be? How broad should be their reach? How do our business and personal Values coexist? What ethical considerations should be taken into account?

We will revisit our benchmark service companies to explore the Values that govern their behavior. This will enable us to demonstrate how these companies rely on attitudes and behaviors to support their Purpose, using real-life examples from your experiences as consumers.

Establishing your Values will be time-consuming. Furthermore, this step in the process requires a great deal of thought, self-examination, and candor. You must discern and articulate those things that matter most to you. Additionally, you must give detailed thought to how your Purpose influences those with whom you serve and interact. These are weighty, but worthy, matters that will require a considerable investment of time.

Beliefs

Let us preface our discussion of Values by establishing the connection between your belief system and your Value system. Beliefs are the foundation upon which your Values are built. Beliefs are a state of mind in which trust or confidence is placed in a person or thing. They are also tenets or bodies of tenets held by a group.

Your belief system is fluid in that it continues to develop. You have formed beliefs throughout all stages of your life, from your childhood to your adolescent and school years to your adult years. These beliefs can be renewed, altered, or completely changed based upon new information and experiences. However, at any given time, you have a series of beliefs to which you adhere.

Take a moment to reflect on your beliefs. It is from these beliefs that your Values will emanate.

Who Establishes Values?

If you are embarking on an individual journey of achieving Service Excellence, it is you who establishes your Values. In this instance, you must take into consideration all the people to whom you are connected: families, colleagues, communities, religious groups, companies, and those you serve. Establishing Values is a thought-provoking process that requires you to discern what matters most to you and, perhaps more importantly, what matters most to others.

If you are part of a team or company that is collectively completing the steps to Service Excellence, every member should participate in establishing Values. As with your Purpose, for Values to have meaning, they should reflect a cooperative effort. We will review techniques for establishing group Values later in this chapter.

How Should Values Be Formed?

Your beliefs will guide you, your experiences will channel your thoughts, what matters most to you will steer you, and your conscience will serve as your filter. At the end of your process, you will have a Value system that is based on doing the right thing for everyone with whom you deal; it is called *ethics*.

How Detailed and Broad Do Values Need to Be?

Your list of Values need not be long, complicated, or expansive. Furthermore, your Values should be stated clearly and concisely so as to be easy to remember. If they are top of mind, there is a greater likelihood that your behaviors will consistently align with your Values.

In today's world, the components of our lives are intertwined, and consequently it is often difficult to compartmentalize our personal and work lives. So the breadth of your stated Values should encompass all aspects of your life and include all of the constituencies with whom you engage. Your Values should direct your behaviors in your personal, business, and community life.

Examples of Values

As promised, we will now revisit our benchmark service companies to examine their Values. Our intent is to tap into your personal experiences with these companies and ask you to identify the behaviors they exhibit in support of their Values. Again, Values guide our behaviors, which enable us to live our Purpose.

• Starbucks Values •

- We provide a great work environment and treat each other with respect and dignity.
- We embrace diversity as an essential component in the way we do business.

- We apply the highest standards of excellence to the purchasing, roasting, and fresh delivery of our coffee.
- We develop enthusiastically satisfied customers all of the time.
- We contribute positively to our communities and our environment.
- We recognize that profitability is essential to our future success.[1]

• Marriott Values •

- The unshakable conviction that our people are our most important asset
- An environment that supports associate growth and personal development
- A reputation for employing caring, dependable associates who are ethical and trustworthy
- A homelike atmosphere and friendly workplace relationships
- A performance reward system that recognizes the important contributions of both hourly and management associates
- Pride in the Marriott name, accomplishments, and record of success
- A hands-on management style—that is, "management by walking around"
- Attention to detail
- Openness to innovation and creativity in serving customers
- Pride in the knowledge that our customers can count on Marriott's unique blend of quality, consistency, personalized service, and recognition almost anywhere they travel in the world or whichever Marriott brand they choose[2]

1 Source: www.starbucks.com/aboutus/environment.asp
2 Source: www.marriott.com/corporateinfo/culture/coreValues.mi

• Ritz-Carlton Values •

I Am Proud to Be Ritz-Carlton

- I build strong relationships and create Ritz-Carlton guests for life.
- I am always responsive to the expressed and unexpressed wishes and needs of our guests.
- I am empowered to create unique, memorable, and personal experiences for our guests.
- I understand my role in achieving the Key Success Factors and creating The Ritz-Carlton Mystique.
- I continuously seek opportunities to innovate and improve The Ritz-Carlton experience.
- I own and immediately resolve guest problems.
- I create a work environment of teamwork and lateral service so that the needs of our guests and each other are met.
- I have the opportunity to continuously learn and grow.
- I am involved in the planning of the work that affects me.
- I am proud of my professional appearance, language, and behavior.
- I protect the privacy and security of our guests, my fellow employees, and the company's confidential information and assets.
- I am responsible for uncompromising levels of cleanliness and creating a safe and accident-free environment.[3]

• eBay Values •

eBay is a community that encourages open and honest communication among all its members. Our community is guided by five fundamental Values:

- We believe people are basically good.
- We believe everyone has something to contribute.

3 Source: http://corporate.ritzcarlton.com/en/About/GoldStandards.htm#credo

- We believe that an honest, open environment can bring out the best in people.
- We recognize and respect everyone as a unique individual.
- We encourage you to treat others the way you want to be treated.[4]

eBay is firmly committed to these principles. And we believe that community members should also honor them—whether buying, selling, or chatting with eBay friends.

• Southwest Airlines •

This very successful company, led for most of its years by Herb Kelleher, does not have a set of published Values. But in Kevin Freiberg and Jackie Freiberg's wonderful book, *Nuts! Southwest Airlines' Crazy Recipe for Business and Personal Success,* we found the essence of their company Values on page 147:

> Unlike many companies, Southwest has never formally documented its principal Values. However, we have identified at least 13 dominant Values that drive the company and contribute significantly to Southwest's corporate character:

1. Profitability
2. Legendary service
3. Low cost
4. Egalitarianism
5. Family
6. Common sense
7. Fun
8. Good judgment
9. Love
10. Simplicity
11. Hard work
12. Altruism
13. Ownership

4 Source: http://pages.ebay.com/help/newtoebay/community_overview.html?

Southwest proudly publishes the following commitment to their employees on the company Web site:

> We are committed to provide our Employees a stable work environment with equal opportunity for learning and personal growth. Creativity and innovation are encouraged for improving the effectiveness of Southwest Airlines. Above all, Employees will be provided the same concern, respect, and caring attitude within the organization that they are expected to share externally with every Southwest Customer.

There are many similarities in the Values of our benchmark companies. They all address concern for one another, the communities in which they operate, and the clients they serve. Most speak to their internal environment, while some touch on their external environment. There are some how-to guidelines, along with diversity, equality, and profitability Values. Common to every company is the sense that these Values come from a foundation of deeply rooted beliefs.

These Values also contain meaningful expressions of personal attributes that we refer to as *traits*. Pride, trust, responsiveness, ownership, and respect are just a few of these. The traits of successful service people are so essential to a company's ability to achieve Service Excellence that we have devoted an entire chapter to this subject later in the book.

It should be noted that these Values can be easily found on company Web sites, in internal communiqués, on signs posted in the workplace, and, in the case of Marriott, Ritz-Carlton, and CROSSMARK, on wallet cards. The Values of successful companies are not closely guarded secrets!

• CROSSMARK •

Let us reengage with the successful CROSSMARK transformation. As Jim Borders, Rob Livingston, and I made our way around the country, the topics of Purpose and Values always generated lively conversation.

We followed the same procedure for establishing Values as we did for developing a Purpose. The audience was divided into 8 to 10 small groups, each of which brainstormed a series of Values. These were then presented to the full audience who, by popular vote, reached consensus on the Values they believed would best guide them toward becoming who they wanted to be.

At the conclusion of these meetings, we had a total of 35 separate lists for submission to CROSSMARK's Steering Committee. The committee then selected the list of Values developed by one of the groups from the Plano headquarters meetings, as follows:

- We always strive to do the right thing.
- We state our expectations openly so that everyone understands the standards expected of all.
- We are proactive and financially disciplined.
- We feel a strong sense of responsibility for our associates and their well-being.
- We are an equal opportunity employer that supports diversity and rewards performance.
- We are a "learning" organization committed to continuous improvement.
- We know we can provide solutions only to those problems we understand; therefore, we listen.
- We share the credit for our successes.
- We believe great achievement comes through teamwork, collaboration, and mutual support.
- We focus on employee development to ensure our long-term success.
- We have an open-door policy for all employees to their managers.
- We realize that some of our best ideas come from the people closest to the situation.

Living Your Values

> The key to values is more how they are practiced than what they say.
>
> —John Morgridge, Chairman Emeritus, Cisco

As was the case with Purpose, our Values can become empty words if we do not put into practice specific behaviors that support them. Our behavior is what brings Values to life. Let us illustrate this point using some of the CROSSMARK Values:

VALUE. We feel a strong sense of responsibility for our associates and their well-being.
BEHAVIOR. I show concern for my fellow associate by completing an assignment on his behalf so that he can attend one of his children's school awards assemblies.

VALUE. We realize that some of our best ideas come from the people closest to the situation.
BEHAVIOR. Once a week, I encourage those who work for me to recommend ideas for resolving a particularly challenging issue.

VALUE. We focus on employee development to ensure our long-term success.
BEHAVIOR. I make certain every new associate understands my role as it relates to what they do.

This focus on behaviors is one of the ways in which great service companies live their Values. At Ritz-Carltons and Marriotts across the country, associates begin each shift with a formal "line-up" during which they discuss various aspects of service. They also use this time to select and then discuss one of the company

Values, and during the discussion, they ask associates to articulate how they personally live that Value. In this forum, they also recognize outstanding behaviors of their employees to illustrate how they bring their Values to life.

Living your Values will be less challenging if you practice the following:

- Be sensitive to recognizing which things you can control and which things you can't; know the difference.
- Stop to take stock of how a Value applies to you and a situation; a Value is a guideline that will direct your behavior.
- Use Values in decision making, resolving conflicts, and brainstorming so that your outcomes will support your Purpose.
- Apply Values equally to everyone throughout the organization. Applying Values consistently will maximize their significance.

Values Come in Many Forms

Values can take many forms, but the three most prominent are these:

1. *Business Values.* What is important to the company? How do we want to be viewed by the company? What can I contribute to their success?
2. *Personal Values.* What is important to me? How do I want to be viewed? What is my role within my circle of family and friends? What Value do I bring to them?
3. *Ethical Values.* How far will I go to get things accomplished? Do I know where to draw the line? What are my company's expectations of me and my teams?

Finally, as we live our Values, we must recognize that conflicts will arise. With the complexity present in so many aspects of our lives, situations will invariably produce conflict. When business, personal, and ethical Values conflict, every effort should be made to adhere to the common Values that govern behavior.

Prioritizing Values will be required often, but how do we set priorities? The answer is to determine what matters most at that time. Different situations will necessitate different priorities and choices.

Some Possible Conflicts of Values

- My career versus my client
- My career versus my company
- My family versus my company
- My family versus my client
- My client versus my colleagues
- My client versus my ethics
- My company versus my ethics
- My company versus my client

In dealing with conflict as it relates to Values, it is essential that you be consistent and follow through. If everyone is not doing the same thing for the same reasons, the foundation erodes. When making decisions, consider the ramifications of poor or poorly applied Values. Can they damage your company, your clients, your team, your family, or yourself? *That was the ENRON story, wasn't it?*

AN EXTRAORDINARY LEARNING

I had been working for the Campbell Soup Company for about a year when I was offered the opportunity to assume the role of account manager for our New York District's largest co-op account. I was told that my promotion was slightly ahead of schedule; therefore, my performance would be carefully monitored. This caveat produced some initial anxiety, but the excitement of the challenge overshadowed my concerns.

On my very first solo call to this account, I was particularly excited to be presenting Campbell's biggest promotion of the year, their "new-pack" tomato soup plan. As was customary, I visited the co-op's warehouse prior to my call to conduct a physical inventory of their tomato-based soups. (These were preautomation days!) Each buyer had been given a stock count prepared by the warehouse manager so, as sales reps, we provided a check on their system.

Upon completing the task, I took my place in the waiting room with the other sales representatives. On this particular day, I was second in line to see the buyer. When it was my turn, I felt a keen sense of excitement as I entered his office. This year the promotion was exceptionally advantageous, and I sensed the buyer would be receptive to my proposal. I was correct. He seemed rather pleased and asked me to continue.

I told him, "Since the quantity of this year's crop translates to a price decline, I will protect the value of your on-hand inventory by sending you a refund check for the amount of the price differential."

He replied, "Well then good, let's get started and determine how much of a refund I will receive for my stock on hand, shall we?"

"All right," I said, and I began to read the inventory counts that I had just completed for each of the tomato-based varieties stocked in his warehouse.

He countered each of my inventory numbers with a number somewhat higher than the actual case quantity I'd recorded just one-half hour earlier. I was perplexed and concerned about this variance, and, with a quick calculation, I determined that this "high count" would net him a reimbursement that was over $3,000 more than his actual warehouse inventory justified.

We completed the list. "Anything else?" he asked, and he then bid me a pleasant good-bye, assuming our business was finished.

I left his office uncertain of my next step and in fear that I would lose the confidence of the company that had just promoted me. Not knowing what to do, I returned to the warehouse and recounted the entire inventory on hand. Then I inquired as to whether there was misplaced stock that I had somehow failed to count.

"No, you got it all," said the warehouse manager. "Every last case was counted."

I returned to the waiting room, hoping the buyer would see me without an appointment so that we could discuss the variance in our numbers. As I waited, I discussed the situation with another sales representative whom I knew quite well. His advice was simple and direct.

"Don't give it another thought, Bob. Take his numbers and go on about your business. This is done all the time. It's part of the cost of doing business."

That just didn't seem right to me. So I stayed in the waiting room the entire day until finally, at five o'clock, the buyer emerged from his office and asked why I was still there.

"I really have to see you about something that's very important, and I couldn't leave until I did."

"Bob," he responded, "that is what we have next week for."

"I can't wait for next week. The situation has me really troubled." So we returned to his office, and we sat across his desk from one another.

He looked at me and asked: "Well, what is it that is so important it can't wait until next week?"

I responded that the inventory count he had given me that morning did not match the actual inventory count in his warehouse.

"So?" He said with a smile.

"So, I can't accept your numbers because, if I did, I would be giving you $3,100 more than you are entitled to, and that just isn't right."

He looked at me with a grim expression, and then he looked down at his inventory records. He asked me to give him the accurate count for each variety. I read my numbers, and he changed all of the quantities on the inventory form to the proper figures. He signed the original, stood up, and handed it back to me.

I took the form and, not knowing what to expect, listened as he went on to say: "Young man, as difficult as it may have been for you to come back here and confront me on that discrepancy, I want you to know you did the right thing. You're new to this business, but as someone who's been at it for a while, I will tell you that took courage."

He went on to say, "If you continue to conduct yourself throughout your career as you did with me today, as difficult as it may be at times, you will have a very successful career."

He reached across his desk, extended both hands, and gave me the warmest and firmest handshake I have ever received.

LESSON TO REMEMBER

At times, living your Values will put you to the test. In those instances, when you are at a crossroads, the way you react will have a significant impact on you and your relationships. If you live your Values, they will guide your behavior. This is what Values do, and you will end up doing what is right.

6

Understand Client Needs

How a company builds and sustains a competitive advantage would depend on how well it delivers on the total consumer experience—cognitive, emotional and behavioral, as desired by the consumer, while meeting its own corporate goals. This report clearly shows that failing to collect and analyze consumer information that highlights key emotive factors present during key interactions is throwing away the opportunity to increase the value of the service and take market share.

—Joby John, Professor and Chair of Marketing
at Bentley College, Boston, Massachusetts[1]

Joby John is referring to an IBM Global Business Services Consumer Experience Survey which found that a mere 17 percent of business leaders consider emotional factors when making consumer-related decisions.

This chapter delves into the concept of client needs and expands on the importance of discerning hard needs from soft needs, as introduced in Chapter 2. To review:

- A *hard need* is satisfied by *what* you do, be it a product or service offering.
- A *soft need* is satisfied by *how* you do what you do—that is, the intangible and emotional connection to what you do.

---

1 Source: IBM press release, 2006, www-3.ibm.com/press/us/en/pressrelease/19600.wss.

A client's soft needs enable the formation of a special connection with that client, but only if you truly understand and can satisfy these intangible and frequently unexpressed needs. Clients have both hard needs and soft needs, so it is critical that you be able to both make the distinction and respect, embrace, and satisfy the unique contribution that each client brings to your relationship. This alone will position you for success and ease some of the stress and anxiety inherent in service relationships.

When a relationship is based solely on *what* you do, never venturing beyond the commercial connection, there is a fairly good chance it will not endure the test of time. During the course of the association, it's quite likely you will encounter situations in which the product or service fails to meet expectations and there will be no special connection to cushion the blow. Then again, if you are one of those rare businesses with little or no competition, I suppose you can choose to do as you please with minimal risk. There is only one Department of Motor Vehicles. But when an alternative comes along . . . beware.

In the first chapter we cited that two out of every three customers leave relationships because of poor attitude or indifference from those who serve. What people perceive as "indifference" may be the failure to behave attentively or the failure to invest the time required to honestly understand what customers want. Clearly, lasting relationships go well beyond the basic needs satisfied by what you do; they require intangible gratification (within the context of the *experience*) in some form. Were that not the case, customers wouldn't leave relationships in such numbers.

Improving the experience of a transaction has remarkable potential in business settings because, when delivered well, it is the bridge to loyalty. By virtue of its intangible nature, this aspect of the relationship experience can be subtle and perhaps elusive. It requires an emotional connection with those you serve. The stronger you make this connection, the more successful you will be in establishing loyalty.

How often have we all failed at or complicated relationships by our inability to appreciate the importance of the experience that good relationships demand? When we refer to the "emotional connection with clients," we do so in its most fundamental form. We are not suggesting that you form a deep personal bond with those you serve. Rather, we are encouraging you to reach beyond the commercial connection of two parties (*what* you do) and broaden the value of your product or service by *how* you do what you do.

Hard Needs versus Soft Needs

Throughout this book we will make reference to the distinction between *hard needs* and *soft needs*. To reiterate, hard needs are satisfied by *what* you do (your product or service). They are tangible and basic, and all of your competitors satisfy them.

Consider the cellular phone companies. They are essentially the same in that they satisfy a clear hard need:

I need to communicate with my family, friends, and colleagues instantly, in all voice and text forms.

This is *what* cell phones do. They fulfill a basic need for communication.

But soft needs are satisfied by *how* you do what you do. They are about the experience, the exciting connection, the intangible. Soft needs provide a unique point of differentiation. More difficult to unearth, the key to discovering soft needs is awareness, discussion, listening, and sensitivity.

In June 2007, with much fanfare and anticipation, Apple introduced their *iPhone:*

I'm impressed with how cool this phone makes me feel. I feel so special, leading edge, connected as never before. I'm so happy to be the first in my group to own an iPhone. This is an experience that is unduplicated.

These were the feelings expressed by people exiting AT&T and Apple stores across the country the day the iPhone was first made available for sale. Consumers were almost giddy about this newest form of "cellular-plus" phones. (Unfortunately, Apple soon compromised the trust of their first adopters by announcing a nearly immediate price reduction.)

If you understand and accept this concept of dual needs, you will approach your service relationships in an entirely different, highly productive manner. If you have not embraced this concept previously, doing so now is absolutely essential to moving forward.

Pragmatically, we doubt that there are many individuals or organizations that disagree with this notion. Realistically, the practices we observe suggest people do not broadly follow this approach.

So we will dispense with further examination of hard needs (our job, our work) and turn our focus to exploring the concept of soft needs.

What Do Those You Serve Really Need?

Frankly, many things, but let's begin by assuming those we serve need to feel . . .

- Comfortable and not pressured
- Appreciated
- Respected
- Listened to

And they need to believe that . . .

- They have your undivided attention.
- You are not judging them.
- You are focused on them.
- You are paying attention to their requests.
- You value them.
- You will live up to their confidence in you.

Let's begin with this list of soft needs. We believe these are fairly universal intangible needs of those we serve. Do you concur? Are these some of the soft needs you perceive vital to satisfying and sustaining your loyal client relationships? We encourage you to make your own list and evaluate the extent to which they intersect. We believe our lists will be comparable.

However, although there may be some relatively universal soft needs, it can be dicey to assume a client's intangible needs are similar to yours or those of other clients. It is therefore imperative that you go directly to the source and discover what matters most to each of the people you serve. For this reason, we advise you to engage in a *soft needs assessment process* with the same energy, resourcefulness, and personal research you would invest in comprehending a client's product or service needs. *Listening* is absolutely essential for understanding all of their needs, tangible and intangible alike.

There is an insightful piece from the University of Minnesota, Duluth, Student Handbook on the difference between hearing and listening:

> *Hearing is simply the act of perceiving sound by the ear. If you are not hearing-impaired, hearing simply happens. Listening, however, is something you consciously choose to do. Listening requires concentration so that your brain processes meaning from words and sentences. Listening leads to learning. Most people tend to the "hard of listening" rather than "hard of hearing."*

Have you noticed aging friends and relatives straining to hear while conversing with others? They are "hard of hearing," which is simply part of the aging process. But in straining to hear, have you observed how well they *listen*? They are not "hard of listening"!

Taking this skill to the next level, we suggest that you not be content with just listening to your clients. You must develop proficiency for *active listening*, which is the ability to comprehend precisely what is important to those with whom you converse. This means listening for content, not delivery; not reacting or overreacting to the message; and not interpreting content but remaining receptive to the ideas expressed. This is active listening. It requires focus and an open mind.

Listening Skills

Once, while moderating a meeting in Phoenix, I was privileged to listen to Nido Qubein, a successful entrepreneur and philanthropist, as he shared his simple approach to active listening. The following is his exercise for evaluating your listening skills. If you are truly an active listener, you should answer yes to each of these 20 questions:

How Well Do You Listen?
1. I enjoy listening to people talk.
2. I encourage other people to talk.
3. I listen, even when I do not particularly like the person talking.
4. The sex of the person talking makes no difference in how well I listen.
5. I listen equally well to a friend, an acquaintance, or a stranger.
6. I put away what I am doing while someone is talking.

7. I look at the person talking.
8. I ignore distractions while listening to a person talk.
9. I smile, nod my head, and otherwise encourage the person to talk.
10. I concentrate on what the person is saying.
11. I try to understand what the person means.
12. I seek to understand why the person is saying it.
13. I never interrupt the person talking.
14. If the person hesitates, I encourage him or her to continue.
15. I restate what the person has said and ask if I got it right.
16. I withhold all judgments about the person's idea or message until I have heard all the person has to say about it.
17. I listen regardless of the person's tone of voice, attitude, or choice of words.
18. I don't anticipate what the person is going to say, I just listen.
19. I ask questions to get ideas explained more fully.
20. I ask for clarification of words I do not understand in their context.[2]

How to Listen

If you wish to discover your clients' soft needs, you must solicit their input and then actively listen to understand what is truly important to them. Listening requires you to stay in the moment, block out distractions, and concentrate on what the person is saying.

The use of probing questions facilitates the quality of dialogue that will enable you to understand your clients' soft needs. Questions prefaced in the following manner prove particularly fruitful:

- What do you think about . . . ?
- What would you suggest . . . ?
- What would your reaction be to . . . ?

2 Source: Nido Qubein's Web site: www.nidoqubein.com/goodlistener.pdf.

- What would happen if . . . ?
- How important is that for you?
- What is your biggest concern about . . . ?
- Can you give me an example of . . . ?
- What do you think is a better way to . . . ?
- What do you like most about . . . ?
- What do you like least about . . . ?
- How can I help improve . . . ?

Open-ended questions such as those listed above encourage discussion by demonstrating a genuine interest in others' opinions and beliefs. Once you've asked such questions, actively listen and probe to ensure you understand the replies. Listen for clues to explore areas of importance. Understand the context of the message. Encourage the sharing of new ideas. Maintain an open mind and avoid making judgments. Do not interrupt or interpret. Resist distractions.

Of course, clients' soft needs don't exist in a vacuum. As you work to understand soft needs, be cognizant of the business and personal environments in which your clients reside.

What are your clients' business environments? Are their workplaces relaxed, fun, and casual, or are they tense, stressful, and formal? What are their challenges? Are they free to express their ideas and opinions? Are their soft needs being met by colleagues? What are their strengths and weaknesses? How will they react to your proposals or suggestions? What are their "hot buttons"? What is their tolerance for pain? Do timelines, budget constraints, and criticisms impact them negatively? How do they view your role? Are you seen as an ally, a threat, or a colleague? How do they perceive their competitors, their own companies, and their specific industry? Are they comfortable in their operating space? What motivates them in business and in life? How do they spend their leisure time? Do they enjoy sports, travel, or spending time with their family?

You will gain a more robust understanding of your clients' soft needs by probing issues such as these and actively listening to their responses.

Recognizing Soft Needs

"He'll see you now but only because he craves attention."

Copyright P. C. Vey. Fortune, March 7, 2005. Reprinted with permission.

The following illustrates ways in which both hard and soft needs are satisfied by a single company or transaction:

Apple sells me computers and peripherals (*hard need*).
They also satisfy my need to be a technological leader among my friends (*soft need*).

Henry & Horne provides all of my accounting services (*hard need*).
They also satisfy my need for confidence, trust, and support (*soft need*).

Michelin sells tires for my car (*hard need*).
They also satisfy my need for safety, reliability, and peace of mind (*soft need*).

State Farm sells me homeowner's insurance (*hard need*).
They also satisfy my need for protection and dependability (*soft need*).

Coldwell Banker sells houses (*hard need*).
They also satisfy my need for independence, comfort, and pride (*soft need*).

Don't just sell me goods and services. Satisfy my *soft* needs for ideals, self-respect, certainty, and confidence. Doing so will keep me coming back.

How to Identify Soft Needs

At this juncture, we recommend that you make a list of your own soft needs as a means of further increasing your comfort level with this concept. Reflect on how your needs are being met, or not, by those with whom you interact. Consider your relationships, and think about which are working well and which are not. Reflect on those who serve you. Why are some connections better than others? We suggest that, in those instances in which you have satisfying relationships, some person or company has connected with your soft needs.

We have compiled an extensive list of the many soft needs you, as an individual, may have. Since these are really quite universal, it stands to reason that your clients will have many of the same soft needs. So it is your responsibility to ascertain which needs your clients feel are the most predominant and significant to satisfy for a lasting relationship.

The following is our list of possible soft needs. However, the soft needs assessments you conduct with your clients will reveal which are most prevalent and which are most important to the individual.

To be trusted and to trust	To have your undivided attention
To be appreciated	To be respected
To be listened to	To not be judged
To be focused on	To be comforted
To be valued	To be supported
To have confidence in you	To be independent

To be recognized	To be informed
To be praised	To experience pleasure
To have peace of mind	To contribute
To feel important	To be proud and to feel pride
To have fun	To be heard
To vent	To be treated fairly
To understand	To be understood
To be involved	To be welcomed
To feel comfortable	To feel significant
To be rewarded	To be happy
To be acknowledged	To be secure
To be consulted	To be needed
To be in charge	To lead or be led
To feel connected	To be engaged

Meeting Internal Needs

Whom else do we serve? Simply put, we serve everyone. We serve our families, our friends, our religious groups, our communities, and our country. In the context of *how* we do *what* we do, we most certainly serve our clients and colleagues.

We have presented a framework for needs identification in the context of our client relationships (external service). But the discussion would not be complete without sharing our point of view on the importance of serving those with whom we work (internal service). Understanding and satisfying the needs of both constituencies is absolutely essential for achieving Service Excellence.

I have yet to find a company that has earned high levels of customer loyalty without first earning high levels of employee loyalty.

—Frederick Reichheld, customer loyalty clairvoyant

Let us refer, once again, to our benchmark companies to illustrate our premise.

Starbucks

> We are known for our coffee, but it's our people that make us famous. The people make us famous because they are always working on relationships.
>
> —Howard Behar, former president of
> Starbucks Coffee Company North America

As a regular customer of Starbucks, I have observed that *how* they do *what* they do is clearly one of the more noteworthy contributions to their overall success story. Just envision their working environment. Depending on the size of the store, there may be anywhere from two to six baristas serving customers. Each has a specific role and set of responsibilities, but together their collective focus is to provide a positive customer experience. That experience is achieved because the baristas are aware of and sensitive to one another's needs; they are respectful of each other, never invalidating a fellow employee; and they are always willing to help one another.

When your internal relationships are satisfying, isn't it normal to reflect your good feelings toward those you serve externally? This reaction, to give what you receive, is almost instinctive.

Starbucks recognizes competitors can replicate products, but they can't replicate people. That's precisely why the company focuses so much attention on the employee experience, because it is employees who create meaningful connections with customers. Many marketers view employee relations as a job solely for human resources—they see employees as tools. But employees—happy, rewarded employees—can work wonders for the company's marketing efforts. There is no better

spokesperson for a company, product, and brand than some-
one who is happy with his job and respected by his employer
and peers. A happy employee will, in turn, make customers
happy.

—*John Moore*, Tribal Knowledge

Wegmans Food Markets

The Northeast is home to one of retail's finest illustrations of the power of understanding the needs of your constituencies. Several years ago I had the pleasure of playing a round of golf with Bob Wegman, who was chairman of the board of Wegmans Food Markets at the time. This 18-hole tutorial was rife with lessons on *how* you do *what* you do, by one of the best practitioners in the country.

Bob Wegman has been quoted as saying, "When I became president of our company in 1950, after working in our stores for a number of years, I was determined to make it a great place to work." He raised salaries, introduced fully paid health-care insurance, offered retirement and 401(k) plans, and instituted an employee scholarship program. Bob reports that, "No matter how much we invest in our people, we get much more in return. When I visit our stores, customers stop me and say, 'Mr. Wegman, you have a great store, but wow, your people are wonderful.'"

Bob Wegman has since passed away, but his son Danny has kept this spirit alive: "We have tried to create an environment where our people's ideas are listened to and where they feel empowered to make decisions that impact their work." At Wegmans, they live by the motto "Employees first, customers second." And has it worked?

Well, for 10 consecutive years, Wegmans has been named to *Fortune* magazine's list of the Top 100 Companies to Work For. *Fortune* has also named Wegmans to its Hall of Fame, and it is one of only two dozen companies that have been on the list since its inception.

Wegmans' consistent performance is a tribute to the culture of this outstanding company. Their internal associates are valued, rewarded, and come first. Their culture breeds the kind of spirit that manifests itself in how they serve their customers. It works.

A FABULOUS LEARNING

When I assumed the sales leadership role at Lipton, one of my primary goals was to find a way to differentiate ourselves from our competition. This certainly wasn't going to be an easy task when you considered some of the exceptional food and beverage companies with whom we competed: Nestlé, Kraft, P&G, Nabisco, Campbell Soup, Quaker Oats, General Mills, Pillsbury, Pepsi, and Coca-Cola. Everyone marketed outstanding brands. We all satisfied the hard needs of retailers by promoting these terrific products.

So we looked at the ways in which we tried to satisfy the retailers' soft needs with our customer entertainment practices, but these didn't stand out either. One of our competitors seemed always to have better box seats at baseball parks, better yardage at football games, or better theater tickets, so we had no point of differentiation in that area either.

Unwilling to let this go, we gathered as a management team to brainstorm ways in which to differentiate ourselves by *how* we did *what* we did. We thought about the soft needs of our customers, as well as our internal colleagues, and we searched for an idea that would be unique and pleasing to everyone. Our brainstorm: an annual Holiday Brunch in December to which our customers, salespeople, *and* their families would be invited!

We selected Tavern on the Green in New York's Central Park as our venue. As luck would have it, the Sunday of our inaugural event coincided with the year's first big snowstorm. So while the glass-enclosed Crystal Room showcased a snowy Central Park scene straight from Currier and Ives, the storm prevented many families from attending. Although the RSVPs had numbered close to 200, only 40 to 50 people were able to make the trek into the city.

Needless to say, I was disappointed by the turnout. And yet I was encouraged by a conversation with Nick D'Agostino, CEO, D'Agostino

Supermarkets, and Henry Johnson, COO, Grand Union. They said, "Don't be discouraged, and don't give up on this idea because of the first year's attendance. You are on to something. This can be the best event we attend each year." So we didn't give up; and they were right. The following year nearly 300 people attended, and for the next several years our holiday celebration became the industry's customer event of the year.

Why were we so successful in differentiating ourselves? Because we included the families of our customers, and we included our *colleagues* and the *families* of our colleagues. We identified and satisfied people's soft needs: to feel special, proud, important, included, and significant, just to name a few.

Capitalizing on our success in New York, we went on to further differentiate ourselves by reaching beyond Lipton's headquarters city to hold similar holiday events at Faneuil Hall in Boston and the Ritz-Carlton in Laguna Niguel, California.

LESSON TO REMEMBER

Lipton became different because we took the time and expended the energy to explore alternatives. Breaking with the ordinary and creating the extraordinary require that you challenge yourself to truly understand soft needs; only then can you achieve genuine differentiation. Once you learn what the soft needs are, go satisfy them and you will be on your way!
Read on . . .

7

Satisfy Client Needs

Seek opportunities to create memories; there are no expiration dates on memories.

This chapter speaks to the *client interaction*. During this fourth step of our process, Purpose and Values intersect with needs. When you begin to consistently satisfy the client's soft needs, *how* you do *what* you do will become your way of life.

Understanding needs is of value in building relationships only when you take the next step to ensure those needs are satisfied. A dynamic awareness of the soft needs of your clients will give you a heightened sensitivity for opportunities to "create memories" during the course of your relationship. If your service actions on their behalf are special, the impressions you create will endure. How you go about creating these memories is at the core of this step toward achieving Service Excellence. Our behavior, which is a reflection of our personal traits, also plays heavily in realizing this goal.

In your personal life and career, you have encountered both good and bad service behavior. I feel certain you have come to understand the basics of satisfying client needs. You know, for example, how quickly to return phone calls, respond to e-mails, and answer client questions. You instinctively solve client issues without delay, and you promptly deliver products or services as requested. You recognize the broadly accepted standards of good service behavior.

That said, it can be beneficial to reinforce the basics of good service behavior during the early stages of your service transformation. To do so, we recommend you undertake the exercise of identifying past and present examples in which you have encountered good and bad service. Identify and evaluate the behaviors; then begin the process of overtly emulating and modeling the good and rejecting the bad.

Reflect for a moment on our discussion in Chapter 1 about our service crisis. Indifferent people, flawed technological solutions, and the off-shoring of service support frustrate and anger people, all the while moving us further from this aspiration of satisfying needs. Instead of enjoying a service experience that is enhanced by good technology, we find ourselves trapped in a horrible technology experience that lacks personal service and doesn't satisfy our needs.

When forced to confront bad behaviors or resolve conflicts with companies with whom you do business, your soft needs for connection, attention, respect, and responsiveness continue to be ignored. The interactive voice-recognition programs are broadly criticized by customers, yet companies seem unwilling to admit these are not laudable service solutions. But are we in a position to criticize if our own personal voice-mail greeting has not been updated since the day we started our job or purchased the phone?

An August 8, 2006, *Wall Street Journal* article by Loretta Chao titled "Stuck in a Phone Tree: Some Companies Try to Make Escape Easier" reports on a grassroots effort to humanize the corporate interactive phone experience, borne out of the mass frustration of consumers everywhere:

> *The creator of Gethuman.com, which lists "cheat sheets" for hundreds of corporate phone trees, will announce a campaign*

that encourages companies to ease the aggravation of using their so-called phone trees. Companies agreeing to follow the "GetHuman Standard" guidelines—which include allowing callers to press "0" or say "operator" to reach a live person, and to press "#" or say "repeat" to replay a menu—will play a special tone, or "earcon," at the beginning of the call, signaling to consumers that the company is in compliance.

Gethuman.com is the outgrowth of a blog authored by Internet entrepreneur Paul English. The blog listed ways to get around a handful of phone trees and grew into a popular Web site by posting submissions from volunteers who tested different methods.

Check it out for yourself.

The purpose of this chapter is to define a service protocol that, when adopted, will foster true differentiation, greater customer loyalty, and competitive advantage. The practice of satisfying needs is essential to establishing this type of highly evolved client relationship. But before we embark on the nine fundamentals of satisfying needs, let's pause for a moment to reflect on the basic requirements of vibrant relationships.

We believe four conditions must exist in order for a relationship to be healthy and successful, to grow and to flourish. Failure to fulfill even one of these will persistently test any bond between the parties:

1. You must genuinely care about the other person in the relationship.
2. You must fully understand and be willing to satisfy his or her needs.
3. You must communicate frequently, honestly, and openly.
4. You must put the other person's needs first.

In a workplace where bad attitudes, egocentricities, and self-serving behaviors are the norm, can what we just proposed work? We think so, as the following stories illustrate.

Los Angeles and New York are enormous, heavily populated cities, and they are home to the largest entertainment centers in our country. Both have vibrant service communities whose infrastructures rely on actors, comedians, and other aspiring artists to function. It's interesting to note that these communities of artists (at times known to possess some of the aforementioned disagreeable traits) do, in fact, serve quite well. I dare say their behaviors are at times quite extraordinary. By night, these artists are employed in various service jobs; by day, they audition for roles and take classes to hone their craft.

Let me profile two exceptional individuals who work in the Los Angeles service industry. Angie Gega is a dancer, actor, and singer. While awaiting her big break, Angie supplemented her income by working in the retail shop of an upscale fitness center during the day and a restaurant at night. Crystal Angel is an actor and comedienne. Crystal serves as a hostess for one of LA's "hottest" restaurants.

• Equinox •

Equinox is an upscale fitness center on Sunset Boulevard in the heart of Hollywood, California. This popular club, with over 50 U.S. locations, is aptly recognized for *what* it does (provides the latest fitness equipment, innumerable exercise classes, and a world-class spa) and for the pleasant atmosphere epitomized by their slogan, "It's not fitness. It's life." Many of the young people who work and train at Equinox are aspiring artists. Their big breaks have yet to be realized, so they earn a living in service jobs while chasing their dreams.

Angie worked in the sports gear shop located in Equinox's facility. I met her when she cheerfully guided my selection of a new headset to one that would best satisfy my "hard needs" for my cardiovascular workout. I was so impressed with the service Angie provided that I asked for her thoughts on the significant role the artist community plays in Los Angeles's service industry. She said she found the experience to be invaluable as she pursued her craft, and she used the service experience not only to supplement her income but also to reinforce her acting skills and education.

When I asked her to elaborate, Angie went on to say, "Well, the goal of good service is not to act, but to behave. Behaving well establishes a connection with people and is real. Acting is assuming the character of someone else; behavior is living the character. In serving, when I interact with people, I make certain I'm behaving and not acting. But my behavior creates a vivid experience for me, which I then apply to my acting."

I found Angie's perception of her role as a service person to be insightful. Satisfying the needs of those you serve cannot be achieved or sustained through just acting the role; rather, you must establish the connection through your behavior and be real.

• Il Sole •

About 300 yards west on Sunset Boulevard is one of LA's hottest restaurants, Il Sole. This enormously popular restaurant has thrived for nine years, which is exceptional in a town where "15 minutes of fame" describes the life cycle of most eateries. Il Sole maintains a loyal clientele of "A List" actors, producers, directors, writers, and business executives. Il Sole has built this faithful following in a trendy and inattentive city by *how* they do *what* they do. Their ability to satisfy the soft needs of a regular clientele (many of whom succumb to Hollywood stereotypes) is truly quite remarkable.

I believe Crystal Angel deserves much of the credit for Il Sole's success, along with the marvelous cast of servers who support her. Crystal has been the restaurant's hostess for the past five years, and she is positively the electricity that fills the room each night. In between auditions, casting calls, and periodic roles, *how* she does *what* she does is extraordinary. In her words, "It's like the performance of a symphony orchestra, and I am the conductor."

Every day at four o'clock Crystal accesses the Il Sole reservation system from home to determine who of their "regulars" will be dining with them that evening. As someone who understands the soft needs of her clientele, she decided long ago that the best approach to satisfying everyone would be to treat them the same but not have it appear as such.

The restaurant holds about 80 people, and they serve anywhere from 160 to 230 people a night. Everyone wants an eight o'clock reservation. "I never want anyone to feel inferior. Nor do I want anyone to feel superior, although the challenge is dealing with those whose superiority is self-proclaimed. Everyone who dines with us wants to feel comfortable and 'part of the scene.' Satisfying those needs is my job."

In hiring servers, Il Sole looks first for attitude, then trains for skill. The restaurant takes great care in training their servers, spending nearly a month doing so. They are taught to help one another, be respectful, ask questions, trust everyone, and remember that the customer is always right. Crystal attributes her success to feeling completely empowered to do "whatever it takes" to keep the room running smoothly. They are well staffed, so she backs herself up with two hostesses, freeing her to mingle and attend to the guests.

Crystal summarizes her approach to service this way: "Great service should define your environment, and your environment should reflect that service . . . always."

With the preceding examples as background, we will now address the nine fundamental behaviors that combine to enable people and organizations to feel autonomous and independent in their servicing approach. Adopting these behaviors will result in the building of an environment in which you can satisfy the needs of those you serve unencumbered by rigid rules of conduct—that is, an atmosphere in which you are free to do "whatever it takes" to satisfy the needs of your clients. As you adopt and practice these skills, you can expect to experience a significant improvement in your ability to satisfy needs.

1. Exceed expectations.
2. Resolve conflicts and solve problems.
3. Handle complaints.
4. Communicate better.
5. Focus on those you serve.
6. Empower everyone: the ability to say "I can."
7. Diffuse situations with difficult people.
8. Manage your time.
9. Preserve trust.

1. Exceed Expectations

This may be the most clichéd expression in the lexicon of Service Excellence language, but there is no denying it remains the desired outcome every time we set out to satisfy needs. So how do you exceed expectations? Quite simply by always being available, customizing how you serve, being easy to deal with, and putting the other person first. Instead of promising more than you can give, give more than you promise.

Always Be Available

Be there to serve clients whenever they need you to be there. The Internet has altered our criterion for availability by enabling companies to have a constant presence with their consumers, "24/7." Reliability and availability are vital. Make sure your client knows you are *cheerfully* available on demand. Companies who have made themselves available when customers need their services include Walgreens, FedEx Kinko's, and Starbucks.

Customize How You Serve

Find or develop solutions that fulfill your individual clients' specific needs. Successful service companies customize their business relationships with clients. They pride themselves on their one-to-one interactions. These organizations value the differences in client needs and respond with customized solutions. Examples of companies that have customized their service offerings include Charles Schwab, eBay, and Marriott.

Be Easy to Deal With

Make doing business with you easy and pleasurable. Assume the burden of inevitable aggravations for your clients. Companies who exceed their clients' expectations do so, in part, by creating experiences that are memorable because of their complete lack of angst. Their delivery of services is always hassle free. Some of the companies that have well-deserved reputations for consistently genial business dealings include Enterprise, Nordstrom, and Southwest.

Put the Other Person First

In the words of Walt Disney, "Seek opportunities to create memories." Don't wait for opportunities to present themselves; seek them out. Put your "guests" first. Give those you serve more than they expect.

Disney is one of the great entertainment companies that have satisfied and delighted families by *how* they do *what* they do for generations now. Their purpose is to exceed expectations at every turn. Every employee, or "cast member" as he or she is called, is trained to spoil the guests, create a wonderful experience, and satisfy the intangible needs of all.

All processes at Disney are in concert, and they constantly strive for perfection. Every cast member, in every location, lives his or her purpose every minute of the day. *That is the magic of Disney.*

2. Resolve Conflicts and Solve Problems

Consider the pearl; this beautiful gem is created in response to an irritation. Similarly, conflicts and problems, when deftly resolved, can produce delightfully memorable client experiences. But unlike a pearl that improves with longer exposure to the irritant, conflicts and problems must be resolved with the utmost of speed.

The similarity between how businesspeople manage conflict and the children's game of "hot potato" is striking. "Pass it on! It's too hot to handle!" How many times have you heard, or possibly uttered, any of the following statements?

I was not in that meeting, so I had no idea what was happening.

I was out of town when that situation developed, so don't ask me.

That is an operational issue; they caused it, so let them fix it.

This is clearly not my responsibility, so I'll need to find whoever owns this.

I am furious about this! I will find out who caused this problem.

This is not a problem; they are overreacting. Just ignore it and it will go away.

There may be no single cause of poor service greater than our inability to resolve conflict.

When conflicts arise, we have an overwhelming tendency to deny them, debate them, shift responsibility for them, place blame for them, or hold our breath and hope they go away. But consider the possibility that there may be no better opportunity to impress clients and exceed their expectations than by quickly resolving their problems.

Sam Walton understood this opportunity, and it became the impetus for his Sundown Rule: "A sense of urgency, a respect for others' time, and the desire to exceed our customers' expectations are all factors that make the Sundown Rule such a vital part of our culture. Observing the Sundown Rule means we strive to answer requests by the close of business on the day we receive them. Whether it's a request from a store across the country or a call from down the hall, every request gets same-day service. It's a rule we take seriously."

Jeff, a Wal-Mart pharmacist in Harrison, Arkansas, is but one example of an associate living the Sundown Rule. One Sunday morning he "received a call at home. He learned that one of his diabetic pharmacy customers had accidentally dropped her insulin down her garbage disposal. Knowing that a diabetic without insulin could be in grave danger, Jeff immediately rushed to the store, opened the pharmacy, and filled the customer's insulin prescription."

> The Sundown Rule was Sam Walton's twist on the adage "Why put off until tomorrow what you can do today?" That rule remains an important part of [Wal-Mart's] culture and is one reason [their] associates are so well recognized for their customer service.[1]

Aside from Jeff's admirable demonstration of adhering to the Sundown Rule, you may have noted he was empowered by Wal-

1 Source: www.walmartstores.com/GlobalWMStoresWeb/navigate.do?catg=256.

Mart to open the store's pharmacy on a Sunday. The practice of empowering people is crucial for effective and timely conflict resolution. At the Ritz-Carlton, their staff is preapproved to resolve a guest's problem with financial remuneration of up to $2,000, should that be the appropriate course of action.

We all encounter problems that are not easily resolved. But by accepting ownership of the problem, collaborating on a solution, taking responsibility for a resolution regardless of fault, and communicating to all during the process, you can actually create a positive experience for those you serve. Always be prepared to resolve conflict by knowing the steps you will take because, unfortunately, there will never be a shortage of problems.

We have found conflict resolution to be less daunting if you approach it as a simple five-step process. And remember, *conflict is nothing more than the difference between what you want to happen and what actually happens.*

Step 1. Understand the Problem
- Stay calm.
- Get all the facts.
- Listen nondefensively.
- Do not make excuses.
- Repeat what happened to assure understanding.
- Show concern.

Step 2. Identify the Cause
- What should have happened?
- What has happened?
- What went wrong?
- How do we avoid a recurrence?
- Take ownership of the problem.
- Take responsibility for the solution.

Step 3. Discuss Possible Solutions
- Ask for the client's ideas.
- Suggest options for a resolution.

- Agree on the best course of action.
- Agree on a deadline.
- Be sure the proper people are involved.

Step 4. Resolve the Conflict
- Act swiftly.
- Eliminate the cause.
- Be sympathetic.
- Be apologetic.
- Ask if the client is satisfied.
- Outline steps to ensure that problem does not recur.

Step 5. Communicate the Solution to All Involved
- Be swift.
- Be accurate.
- Be complete.

When we are empowered to resolve conflict, we can act decisively with a sense of ownership, and amazing things can happen!

- A negative can become a positive.
- Discomfort can become pleasure.
- Your client will feel valued and respected.
- Your value to your client will be strengthened.
- You and your company will earn respect for new solutions.

3. Handle Complaints

My experience indicates that most complaints do have some validity and that complaints can be an "early warning system" of conflict on the horizon, and an accurate one at that. When you view complaints in this capacity, they can actually become your ally, enabling you to get ahead of problems and minimize their impact. Conversely, complaints that go unattended generally evolve into conflicts that, in hindsight, could have been avoided. Thus, you should handle complaints immediately and in the following manner:

- Listen carefully and make sure you fully understand the client's complaint before trying to effect a resolution.
- Apologize to the complaining client even if the problems are not your fault.
- Request a second chance to satisfy the client.
- Take complaints professionally, not personally.
- Value complaints as an opportunity to understand where things are going awry and as an indicator of areas that need improvement.
- View complaints as opportunities to strengthen loyalty or win back the customer.

Complaints and conflict create discomfort for everyone. Dissatisfied clients can be extremely difficult to manage. In this environment, *how* you do *what* you do is particularly important. Discipline yourself to remain calm but not detached. Your client most likely needs to vent, which is fine, but remember that your composure can be contagious. Never escalate the situation by using emotionally charged phrases such as "it's our policy" or "no one else has complained."

When you sense it's time for rational conversation, ask your client for suggestions on how to deal with the problem. Many clients appreciate being part of the solution, although others may view it as your sole responsibility. Prepare yourself for the possibility that you may have to "agree to disagree" with your client. Should that happen, immediately and *personally* inform your client (not via an e-mail or letter) of the decision. Be brief and to the point; be empathetic and fair; be apologetic for the condition that caused the problem; and ask for another opportunity to serve your client better in the future.

Proactively resolving complaints is always the right thing to do. But do we always follow this rule?

When conflicts arise, what should you do? A study conducted by the W.P. Carey School of Business at Arizona State University (ASU), in conjunction with the Customer Care Alliance, found that resolving conflicts with clients should not be that difficult since

- 73 percent wanted an explanation of why the problem occurred.
- 71 percent wanted a thank you for their business.
- 70 percent wanted assurance that the problem wouldn't happen again.
- 59 percent wanted an apology or a chance to vent.
- 15 percent wanted revenge.

Curious as to how the companies responded to these client complaints, ASU conducted a follow-up study to answer that very question. So how did those companies resolve conflict?

- 40 percent of the companies did nothing in response to the complaints they received.
- 25 percent apologized.
- 18 percent explained why the problem occurred.
- 18 percent offered refunds.
- 16 percent assured the customer that the problem wouldn't happen again.

How disappointing! Forty percent of the companies involved did not respond to the complaints, and only 25 percent apologized. Is it any wonder why we have a service crisis in America?

So be a hero! The person you rescue from their discomfort may very well view your efforts as heroic. Never run from complaints or conflicts. Embrace them as opportunities to shine in your client's eyes. Be empowered to resolve conflicts. Adopt Nordstrom's "whatever it takes" approach, the Four Seasons' "recovery" philosophy, or the Ritz-Carlton's endorsement of every associate to resolve complaints.

In these difficult times, most organizations practice regular safety and rescue drills to ensure that everyone will be prepared in the event of a disaster. Adopt that same approach with your business. Have periodic "emergency drills" with your team. Be certain everyone knows what to do and how to behave when a difficult situation arises. You too can be ready for the unexpected.

4. Communicate Better

Thousands of books and articles have been written on the subject of good communication skills, yet these skills still continue to elude us. Indeed, rare is the individual or company who couldn't practice better communication skills, both internally and externally. This is particularly true in service situations. Reasons for this dearth of communication are numerous, but significant improvements can come from following just three simple guidelines: be timely, respectful, and perceptive.

Timely Communication

- Communicate at the clients' convenience, not yours.
- Be readily accessible; respond promptly.
- Plan frequent and regular communications.
- Schedule lengthy and important communications well in advance.
- Establish agendas with meeting durations.
- Always follow up.

Respectful Communication

- Be considerate of limitations.
- Avoid taboo topics (religion, politics, and so on).
- Listen more than you talk.
- Be polite, professional, and genuine.
- Never be dismissive or arrogant.

Perceptive Communication

Ask questions that spur dialogue. The more the other person talks, the more you'll learn. Continue questioning until you understand and have uncovered all the information required to proceed. Questions prefaced in the following ways typically generate the most productive communication:

- What do you think about . . . ?
- What would you suggest . . . ?
- What would your reaction be to . . . ?
- What would happen if . . . ?
- How important is that . . . for you?
- What is your biggest concern about . . . ?
- Can you give me an example of . . . ?
- What do you think is a better way to . . . ?
- What do you like most/least about . . . ?
- How can I help improve . . . ?

Never jump to conclusions when communicating with those you serve. Follow the simple technique of "probe, clarify, and validate" to ensure you are obtaining complete and accurate information.

Probe
Q. Are you satisfied with the recommendations in
   the report?
A. Mostly.

Q. Which recommendations are still of concern to you and why?

A. Just the recommendation about timing. I think it's too aggressive.

Clarify

Q. Is it only moderately aggressive? Would you be comfortable if we were to add a week?

A. Yes, that would be great.

Validate

Q: So we will change the timing from August 1 to August 8. Is that acceptable?

A: Yes.

In conversation it is easy to be derailed by a person's delivery, but you must focus on the content of the person's message if you are to discern what is really important to him or her. Do not overreact or react negatively; just accept what is being said. In other words, *be an active listener.*

An Active Listener	*A Passive Listener*
Does not tolerate distractions	Is easily distracted
Allows you to finish	Interrupts the speaker
Participates	Daydreams
Is engaged	Exhibits no energy
Is a respectful communicator	Does not make eye contact

Nonverbal Communication

When communicating with those you serve, observe their nonverbal signals. Take note of their body language, appearance, and posture. Look for signs of distraction. Pay attention to their facial expressions and eye contact; are they signaling emotions about this connection? Listen to the tone of their voice as a means for understanding what they may be *feeling*.

Listening is not merely not talking, though even that is beyond most of our powers; it means taking a vigorous, human interest in what is being told us.

—Alice Duer Miller (1874 to 1942),
American poet and author

5. Focus on Those You Serve

The main thing is to keep the main thing the main thing.

Stephen Covey, *The 7 Habits of Highly Effective People*

You are very busy; you lead a complex and challenging life. You're pulled in countless directions with everyone clamoring for your attention. We have advocated that in order to be successful, you must put the client first. In reality, our lives don't always permit this to happen. At any given time, you may have so many "firsts" in your life that it can seem impossible to meet everyone's needs. Perhaps you feel yourself falling short of your own expectations.

There are many constituents in your life, all of whom can be demanding: external and internal clients, family and friends, and community. Everyone is shouting for your attention, and you find yourself conflicted about who should be first. How do you make certain all of your "firsts" are served when they should be?

The answer is *focus.*

Be completely present at a specific moment in your life . . . at the precise time you are supposed to be there. This delicate maneuver calls to mind another of my favorite circus performers, the magical clown. This clown brilliantly balanced a dozen spinning plates on the end of a stick, never allowing any to fall or break. How did he accomplish this amazing feat? Focus!

The circus metaphor of spinning plates no doubt resonates, given the challenges we all face. As a backdrop to the idea of focus, revisit our discussion of Values. Recall that, in times of conflict, you must rely on the rule of "first things first." While multitasking may seem an appropriate solution to competing obligations, its very nature precludes our ability to focus. Who among us hasn't read and responded to e-mails during a conference call? Were you fully focused on either task?

I recently encountered a clever saying that applies to our topic of focus: "You can always divide your time, but you should never divide your attention."

Focus is about staying in a moment. Focus requires discipline and practice. When you are capable of barring all distractions from "a specific moment," you are on the right path. Your focus is a tangible demonstration of a person's importance to you. You do not allow interruptions to break your concentration. You actively listen and observe; you are engaged. Physical indications of focus (closing your door for meetings, holding all phone calls, honoring scheduled visits) satisfy the soft needs of those you serve—to be acknowledged, respected, listened to, and feel important.

During my tenure at Lipton, I had the privilege of working with our CEO, Hu Tibbetts. He was a master of focus with his ability to maintain concentration on a person or subject. We would meet periodically, and for that time, be it several minutes or several hours, he would not allow his attention to be broken. This focus made me, and others with whom he met, feel special and important. Those moments, regardless of frequency, validated the role and significance of everyone with whom he engaged. It was truly a great privilege and honor to know, work with, and learn from him.

• Tiger Woods •

Tiger Woods and his many accomplishments never cease to amaze me. What makes him so special? I have yet to observe many other professional athletes who maintain his intense level of focus. Other players are concentrating on the golf course; announcers and spectators are concentrating on Tiger; and he is blocking out all distractions to stay in the moment and focus on the shot.

Tiger has achieved luminary status in his sport, with 81 career tournament wins, 61 PGA wins, and 13 major championships through 2007. He is a great philanthropist. He is one of America's leading "brands," lending his name to many world-class products and companies. He is a husband and new father, adding personal dimensions to his busy life. The success he achieves in pursuit of Jack Nicklaus's major championship record will be determined, in part, by how well he divides his time—but not his attention. I suspect Tiger Woods will not only successfully serve the needs of all the "firsts" in his life but also go on to be the greatest golfer of all time.

6. Empower Everyone: The Ability to Say "I Can"

Too often, good service falls victim to bureaucracy. Our ability to serve is constrained by the need for "corporate approval." To succeed as individuals or teams, we must be empowered to serve on the spot. This is the ability to say "I can" rather than "I'll have to check."

It is important to note that we're not suggesting an environment of anarchy, in which everyone can make any decision he or she so chooses. Empowerment requires a firm grounding in your company values, an understanding of management's desires, consistency of direction, and team unity. Common sense and reason must prevail. With this foundation, empowerment will facilitate flexibility, speed, and creativity, culminating in Service Excellence.

The U.S. military has empowered their field personnel to make spur-of-the-moment decisions, but those decisions must be aligned with the military's overall objectives. This means that front-line strategies and tactics are made by privates, not generals. Imagine the carnage from a system in which privates had to check with their superiors before making a decision?

You can be empowered in two ways. The first, and more traditional means, is by the authority inherent in your position or role within the company (the *Rule of Empowerment*). The second, and our challenge to you, is by taking the initiative and accepting accountability to empower yourself (the *Responsibility of Empowerment*). When you consider that empowerment is really about creatively solving problems, capitalizing on opportunities to exceed expectations, and choosing to serve proactively, who would deny you the chance to empower yourself? Remember, in an ideal service environment, we are all equal.

Leadership is the responsibility of every member on a client service team. Associates who understand this consistently empower themselves, making everyone's job easier. They take the initiative to solve problems, even when it's "not their job." They don't play hot potato with clients or issues. They react quickly and decisively when opportunities arise to exceed expectations. Are you one of these people? How would you answer the following questions? How would those you serve and the people on your team answer these questions about you?

- Is your attitude "Yes I can," or is it "Let me check with someone"?
- Are you tireless, with the attitude "I will not rest until this is resolved"?
- Do you constantly strive to make life easier for those you serve?
- When presented with a suggestion, do you follow through or let the idea die?
- Do you ask others for assistance when you don't have an answer, or do you let the matter go unattended?

7. Diffuse Situations with Difficult People

There is no escaping it: you will encounter difficult people. But even difficult people have needs (perhaps more than most?) and they must be satisfied. Emotions govern much of their behavior, so it's imperative that you remain calm, careful, and tactful, particularly in the midst of their fury.

Be smart, but cautious, about how you respond. Remember, "I'm sorry" is not an admission of guilt but a concern for the other person's predicament. Express empathy: "I understand how you feel. I would feel the same way. Let's find a solution." Ask yourself what soft needs are not being met. Move beyond the material facts of the situation.

We have found certain phrases to be most effective when attempting to diffuse a difficult situation:

- How may I help you?
- Thank you so much for your patience and cooperation.
- I'm so sorry to hear that; I don't blame you for being frustrated.
- Let's work together to make this right, shall we?
- I understand why you feel that way. It must be upsetting.
- I understand what went wrong; we will make sure it never happens again.
- What can I do to make you feel better about this?

Conversely, certain phrases should be avoided at all costs:

- Our policy is . . .
- Calm down!
- What's your problem?
- That's not our fault!
- It's not my responsibility (or job).
- I'm not going to repeat this again . . .

- I'm really busy right now.
- Listen to me . . .
- I can't . . .
- Why don't you be reasonable?
- There's nothing else I can do . . .

Is the client *always* right? Perhaps not, but the client *always* wins. So view complaints as opportunities and allies. Prioritize client needs over yours. And remember, perception is reality. If those you serve feel they are receiving poor service, then they are receiving poor service. So who is the boss in our service relationships?

> There is only one boss—the customer. And he can fire every-body in the company from the chairman on down, simply by spending his money somewhere else.
>
> —Sam Walton, Wal-Mart Founder

Dan Lueders, my trademark attorney, shared this story about one of his partners in Indianapolis, Tom Henry. Tom went into a local bagel shop and ordered a bagel with multiple toppings in a particularly detailed and fussy way. The proprietor politely began to prepare the bagel when Tom, somewhat embarrassed by his high-maintenance order, apologetically said, "I know, I know, the customer is always right." The proprietor responded, "No, the customer is always the customer."

Clients haven't cornered the market on difficult people; you will encounter them within your own organization as well. Managing internal conflict and handling highly charged situations with supervisors can be very challenging. How you say things is as important as what you say. Be cognizant of your timing, and respect the chain of command. Use the language and tools we have discussed; they are not exclusive to client interactions.

In an ideal service environment, everyone would feel free to discuss matters of service. If that doesn't exist in your organization or team, you can help create this atmosphere by having the personal courage to express your beliefs in order to seek improvement or correct deficiencies. Your approach, *what* you say and *how* you say it, will be especially important if this kind of open discussion is in its infancy. "I could use some guidance with . . . ," or "It would be helpful to me if . . . ," or "I want to do this better and I need your assistance" sounds much better than "If you would only . . . ," or "I'm sick and tired of . . . ," or "You always . . ." Think about how you would like to be approached, and use that as your guide.

The Language of Service

Say This	*Not This*
Certainly	Okay, sure
I would be happy to	Whatever
It would be my pleasure	I guess so
Good morning	Hey!
May I place you on hold?	Hold on

Your Values and Difficult People

Being a *server* does not mean being a *servant*. Servants do exactly as they are told; servers do the right thing. As a server, you should never sacrifice your values or personal integrity. "Doing what is right" should govern your actions. Model behavior will earn you the respect of your clients, so never compromise your own beliefs. Do not tolerate personal affronts; if you respect yourself, others will as well, even the most difficult of people.

8. Manage Your Time

Time management is a subject that has spawned entire books, seminars, and businesses. Yet we wonder if people have availed themselves of the myriad tools available because we continue to hear that one of the reasons people do not serve well is they "don't have the time." Our response, shocking and perhaps a bit heretical, is this: *You can always find the time to do what is important.* It is not a matter of time; it is a matter of desire.

• Microsoft •

In 2005, Microsoft conducted the "Microsoft Office Personal Productivity Challenge (PPC)," which drew responses from more than 38,000 people in 200 countries. The intent of the survey was to rate workers' productivity based on their responses to statements about work-related practices. Many of Microsoft's findings, similar to the two below, support our premise regarding time and desire.

1. In the United States, of the 45 hours in an average workweek, 16 were unproductive.
2. In the United States, the most common productivity pitfalls were procrastination (42 percent), lack of team communication (39 percent), and ineffective meetings (34 percent).

The PPC survey also identified "time wasters," defined as things that prevent people from doing something of more value and importance. We're certain these will look familiar:

- Interruptions from coworkers
- Unproductive meetings
- Unexpected visitors
- Personal phone calls
- Inability to say no[2]

You will note that this study didn't address the time at work spent shopping online or surfing the Web for personal reasons, which we know from other surveys to be significant.

---

2 Source: www.microsoft.com/presspass/press/2005/mar05/03-15threeproductivedayspr.mspx.

To help control your time and eliminate waste, be sure to utilize the following basic time management guidelines:

- Set deadlines to ensure that you meet your service objectives.
- Prioritize and record your tasks.
- Prioritize your clients and projects by establishing "tiers."
- Use planning tools and Service Action Plans to meet goals (Chapter 8).
- Delegate for assistance, not for "buck passing."

9. Preserve Trust

Trust is a firm belief in the reliability, truth, ability, or strength of someone or something.

—*The New Oxford American Dictionary*

Why would anyone enter a relationship with someone he or she did not trust? Isn't trust a prerequisite for an engagement to occur? Trust is the essential underpinning of any service relationship, so it follows that it is yours to preserve *or* lose.

However, there are degrees of trust owing to factors like time, experience, and behavior. In a service relationship, you have the exceptional opportunity to reinforce and strengthen the trust bestowed upon you by *how* you do *what* you do. You must be consistently truthful, reliable, and capable, and in so doing, you will preserve and build the trust of those you serve.

On Becoming a Trusted Partner

If you serve your clients well, you will be respected, valued, and relied upon; ideally, you will attain the status of *trusted partner*.

You need just summon your early life lessons to recognize the behaviors of a Trusted Partner (hence, the similarity of this list to the Boy Scout Law). These are traits of exemplary service people, which is the subject of Chapter 9:

Be always truthful.	Be complete.
Be ever reliant.	Be forthright.
Be always respectful.	Be sensitive.
Be unselfish.	Be communicative.
Be humble.	Be proactive.
Be timely.	Be responsive.
Be accurate.	Be accessible.

Understanding and practicing the nine fundamentals of satisfying needs, and adopting them as a form of organizational protocol, will put you well along the path of your service transformation. Use this chapter as your guide to behavior modification, both personally and organizationally, should you determine certain behaviors are standing in the way of progress. The importance of this fourth step on the roadmap to Service Excellence cannot be overemphasized, nor can it be tabled if you have any hope of success.

A WONDERFUL LEARNING

In the mid-1990s, I relocated from Chicago to Scottsdale, Arizona. As moves go, it was relatively easy; I left my "city" apartment and furniture behind and found a new home with the more casual look of the Southwest. With little unpacking to do, I quickly set about tending to the dry-cleaning and tailoring needs of my wardrobe.

Two pairs of slacks needed alterations, so one of my new neighbors directed me to a little shop in the nearby strip mall, owned by a woman named Gerda. In a matter of minutes, I had pulled into the parking space directly in front of Gerda's shop, where I observed a rather large sign in the window that read:

> WE ARE CLOSING ON WEDNESDAY FOR TWO WEEKS OF VACATION.
> PLEASE BE CERTAIN TO PICK UP YOUR CLOTHES BY THEN.

This was Friday afternoon, just a few business days before the shop would close for two weeks. Overcome by anxiety (yes, over slacks), I raced into the shop, ignored Gerda's genial welcome, and blurted "I see from the sign in the window you're leaving for vacation, and I have two pairs of slacks that I desperately need altered. Can I have them by Wednesday?"

Graciously overlooking my lack of pleasantries, Gerda smiled warmly and replied, "Well, of course you can have them by Wednesday, but why do you want to wait so long?"

Confused by this, I asked "What? What do you mean, why do I want to wait so long? When can I have them?"

Gerda inquired about my plans for the next afternoon: "Where will you be?"

"Where do you want me to be?" I sheepishly asked.

"Be here at two o'clock and your slacks will be ready."

LESSON TO REMEMBER

Service Excellence requires that you seek opportunities to create memories, then act on those opportunities. Gerda not only (cheerfully) satisfied my needs by ensuring my slacks would be altered prior to her vacation, she also recognized an opportunity to create a vivid memory. Because of *how* she did *what* she did, I remained Gerda's loyal customer all the years I lived in Scottsdale.

8

Create a Service Action Plan

Creating your Service Action Plan is the fifth step on our road-map to Service Excellence. To understand what we mean by *Service Action Plan*, you need look no further than the glove box of your automobile. Your owner's manual contains a detailed maintenance plan with the service and timing requirements to ensure maximum performance of your vehicle. Adhering to this Service Action Plan satisfies the soft needs of drivers to feel safe, secure, and conscientious.

Another great example of a Service Action Plan is the bestselling book *YOU: The Owner's Manual: An Insider's Guide to the Body That Will Make You Healthier and Younger*, published in 2005 by Michael F. Roizen, M.D., and Mehmet C. Oz, M.D. This "insider's guide" simplifies and explains the complexities of the human body; but it also provides very specific plans for maximizing your health and longevity.

The following year, this trusted medical team published *YOU: On a Diet: The Owner's Manual for Waist Management*. In their opening chapter, the good doctors "give you everything you need to make a body change—through a series of elegant and effective changes based on hard science—that will stick with you for your life. Simply, this book will serve as your lifelong waist management, body-changing plan." Direct enough?

Building on the success of these first two Service Action Plans for the human body, Drs. Roizen and Oz published their third book in 2007, *YOU: Staying Young: The Owner's Manual for Extending Your Warranty*. There must be something to this Service Action Plan concept!

Service Action Plans, whether they be for your automobile, body, or client relationships, are designed to lay out specific actions and corresponding timetables that, when followed, enhance satisfaction, performance, and longevity.

The plan you develop for your service relationships should be a *written document* that can be shared, referenced, monitored, and measured. This document will guide your behavior and provide a structure within which to operate. We do not recommend a lengthy tome with pages upon pages of detailed action plans; you are busy enough. Rather, your Service Action Plan should be a very simple and straightforward document.

A Sample Service Action Plan

The Service Action Plan examines three interrelated questions. A separate plan should be prepared for everyone you serve, be it an individual or a constituency:

1. *Who is being served?* Identify the person or constituency to whom you are providing service. Remember to include both internal and external clients.
2. *What are your clients' soft needs?* List your clients' soft needs, ascertained during the needs assessment stage of your roadmap to Service Excellence (step 3). Record only their soft needs, not their hard needs (Chapter 6).
3. *What service actions will satisfy your clients' soft needs?* Detail the service actions that will satisfy the soft needs of the people you are serving. Your service actions must be specific, time bound, and measurable in regard to results and impacts.

In the early stages of your service transformation, we suggest writing your Service Action Plan on a 5- by 7-inch index card for portability and ready reference. On the front, list your Purpose and Values; this will prove helpful until such time as they are committed to memory. On the back, identify those you are serving, their soft needs, and your planned action steps to satisfy those needs.

SERVICE ACTION PLAN

Purpose:

Values:

Front

Who is being served?

Needs:

Service actions:

Back

Why a Written Plan?

Before we review sample Service Action Plans, we need to discuss the reasons why it is important to put your plans into writing. First and foremost, a well-written plan significantly increases your chances of satisfying the needs of your client and receiving recognition for doing so. Many years ago I was taught the following:

- In the absence of a well-defined, written plan, you have a 30 percent chance of receiving high marks from your client.
- With a general plan in place, you have a 50 percent chance of receiving high marks from your client.
- When you have a detailed, mutually agreeable, broadly communicated plan with standards and measures, you have a 90 percent chance of receiving high marks from your client.

It's difficult to fathom launching a major initiative, new product, fiscal year, or new company without a written business plan. You would be denied funding, support, and people; it would be disastrous. Business plans are complex, and they can take many months to prepare depending on their scope and duration. But they are vital tools for success, guiding your business decisions, measuring your progress, and providing a framework for course corrections.

Your Service Action Plan is every bit as important as your business plan. Just as you develop plans for financial success, the Service Action Plan positions you for relationship success. However, it doesn't require nearly the preparation time as does a business plan. Service Action Plans are fashioned by an individual for an individual, by a team for a team or an individual, or in the case of large-scale engagements, by a company for a client.

A Service Action Plan guarantees that you and your team have defined and agreed upon what is important when serving clients and one another. It establishes a common ground for communicating with others who serve the same individual or team. Additionally, a written Service Action Plan is the ideal framework for companies to keep abreast of how their associates are serving one another and their external clients.

Whom Do I Serve?

On the surface, this question appears to be exceedingly simple. But consider, for a moment, an average workweek and the countless interactions required to keep your company, clients, and relationships moving forward. The following chart depicts the many possibilities for service relationships in a typical organization. Clearly you collaborate with management, peers, direct reports, and, most certainly, your clients. Are there others?

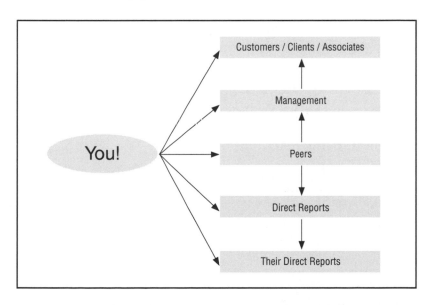

At the outset of CROSSMARK's service transformation, it was fairly typical for their associates to create anywhere from three to five Service Action Plans. In general, these plans were developed for constituencies (for example, a client organization or an internal functional group) rather than individuals. This was a valuable first step as it allowed them to isolate groups of people based solely on the nature of their service relationships and determine the communal needs of each group. As their comfort level and appreciation for the power of this process grew, they evolved to service action planning for specific individuals.

Identifying Soft Needs and Service Actions

Chapter 6 was devoted to clarifying the difference between hard needs and soft needs. Business and account plans are typically the domain of hard needs, which are satisfied by the work you perform on behalf of your clients (*what* you do). Service Action Plans are the province of soft needs, which are satisfied by *how* you do *what* you do. The service action segment of your plans should describe the behaviors necessary to satisfy a client's soft needs.

To illustrate this concept, we have created two examples of Service Action Plans for *client constituencies* (as opposed to individuals). Example 1 addresses an internal client group, and example 2 addresses an external client group.

Example 1: Service Action Plan for an Internal Client Group

Who Is Being Served?
An internal department

Soft Needs
To feel secure in their role

To feel valued by the company

To feel respected and important

To be proud of their company

To be treated fairly

To receive timely communications regarding company changes

To be listened to

Service Actions

Publicly recognize the group's top performer each week.

Provide a monthly financial update to the group.

Return all calls and e-mails the same day they are received.

Provide personal feedback via phone calls each month.

Provide a forum for two-way exchanges on issues of concern.

Example 2: Service Action Plan for an External Client Group

Who Is Being Served?

An external client group

Soft Needs

To feel like an important client to your company

To be heard; to be given the opportunity to vent when problems occur

To be informed

To have senior management involvement in their business

Service Actions

Call the client's "relationship owner" a minimum of once a month to ask for feedback and *listen*.

Send a personal update on the company and team once a quarter.

Return all calls from the client organization within the same day; resolve any issues within 24 hours.

Attend all senior leadership meetings, as scheduled.

Create an opportunity to interact socially with the client at least once a year.

As with the CROSSMARK experience, it is beneficial to begin the practice of developing Service Action Plans by focusing on constituencies rather than individuals. This enables you to gain comfort with the process, reinforce your understanding of its role in serving clients, exercise your ability to distinguish between hard and soft needs, and link service actions to need satisfaction. However, Service Action Plans are significantly more compelling when developed for specific individuals. Do not lose sight of the end goal to make the transition to individual Service Action Plans as quickly as possible.

We have continued to emphasize the tenet that we are all equal in matters of service. As you answer the first question of this process ("Who is being served?"), you will find that the same individual or constituency very likely appears in many of your colleagues' plans. This presents a tremendous opportunity to collaborate with your peers on accurately defining soft needs and creating reciprocal service actions. In so doing, your chances of satisfying the needs of those you serve increase exponentially. The power of this collaborative approach to Service Action Plans cannot be overemphasized.

In his book *The Wisdom of Crowds*, Jim Surowiecki reinforces this point:

> *I think the most important lesson is not to rely on the wisdom of one or two experts or leaders when making difficult decisions. That doesn't mean that expertise is irrelevant, or that we don't need smart people. It just means that together all of us know more than any one of us does.*
>
> *There are four key qualities that make a crowd smart. It needs to be diverse, so that people are bringing different pieces of information to the table. It needs to be decentralized, so that no one at the top is dictating the crowd's answer. It needs a way of summarizing people's opinions into one collective verdict. And the people in the crowd need to be independent, so that they pay attention mostly to their own information, and not worrying about what everyone around them thinks.*

Additional Thoughts on Developing the Service Action Plan

- *Involve everyone who can make a contribution.* We cannot underscore this point enough. The more people who participate in the process, the better your chances are of more fully understanding needs, developing robust Service Action Plans, and ultimately succeeding.
- *Have an informal meeting with the person you are serving.* Share your thoughts on the soft needs you perceive to be important, and confirm the accuracy of your views. Make certain the person understands that the conversation is *solely* about understanding and satisfying his or her needs. Think about this! You are embarking on a mission of service. By making time to have this conversation, you're demonstrating how essential it is that the person you are serving be satisfied by *how* you do *what* you do.
- *Be thorough and creative in your service actions.* Go beyond the basics. Don't limit your success by being ordinary; aspire to be extraordinary. Make your service actions special. Recall our discussion about seeking opportunities to create memories? If you *plan* to create memories, you will.
- *Be relentless in unearthing all of your client's soft needs.* Using the feedback techniques suggested earlier, probe, validate, and confirm to uncover your client's hidden needs. These will be the "keys to the kingdom" in forming exceptional service relationships.
- *Create Service Action Plans that are explicit and contain milestones for success.* The specificity of your plans will signal a complete understanding of the soft needs and enable measurement. Timing and success milestones motivate the execution of plans, and they provide a means for measurement as well.
- *Solicit feedback about your Service Action Plan's design and content.* Look to your internal and external clients, peers,

and associates for this input. Discuss your plans with the leaders in your company; again, since we are all equal in service matters, it is incumbent upon everyone to share, advise, contribute, and champion the mission.

Service Action Plan Evolution

By its very nature, a Service Action Plan must be fluid. As your experience uncovers new needs, and formerly remarkable interactions become routine, it is imperative that your service actions evolve in order to remain on an uninterrupted trajectory toward ever-higher levels of client satisfaction.

Unleashing the full potential of the Service Action Plan resides in your ability to hone your plans from a constituency down to an individual. However, there are circumstances in which the constituency is so large it would be impractical to create individual Service Action Plans. In instances such as these, we recommend creating a group plan to address their communal needs, and individual plans for those within the group who, for reasons of role or special needs, will benefit from separate handling.

Regardless, you will find that as your comfort level with Service Action Plans grows, your action plans will naturally morph from groups to individuals and from generalities to specifics.

Let us now review three examples of CROSSMARK Service Action Plans, one each for an external *individual* client, an internal *individual* associate, and an internal *group* of retail representatives.

CROSSMARK Example 1: Service Action Plan for an External Individual Client

At CROSSMARK, account executives (AEs) have responsibility for managing the company's relationships with clients such as Nestlé. There are roughly 200 AEs at CROSSMARK, each of whom interacts with people on the client side and numerous internal associates. This first illustration is a Service Action Plan written by a CROSSMARK AE for a specific individual at the client organization.

Who Is Being Served?
Client (individual person)

Soft Needs
To feel important to CROSSMARK

To be listened to, and heard

To be given the opportunity to vent when problems occur

To be informed

To be the AE's focus

To receive prompt responses

Service Actions
Schedule quarterly feedback sessions to discuss areas for improvement.

Promptly return all calls from client (minimum requirement is same day).

Resolve all issues within 24 hours.

Create a weekly report addressing pertinent industry-related issues.

Identify creative ways to provide reports (minimum semi-annually).

Invite client to be a member of CROSSMARK's client advisory panel.

CROSSMARK Example 2: Service Action Plan for an Internal Individual Associate

Within the CROSSMARK organization, the account executive relies heavily on the administrative assistant and vice versa. Service reciprocity is customary, to some degree, in all companies.

In these circumstances, hierarchies and job roles define *what* a person does, but recall that in matters of service, everyone is equal. This second illustration is a Service Action Plan written by a CROSSMARK AE for a specific individual (administrative assistant) within the company.

Who Is Being Served?
CROSSMARK administrative assistant (individual person)

Soft Needs
To be informed

To be empowered

To be listened to, and heard

To be appreciated

To feel included

To feel important

To be understood

Service Actions
Provide all reports one day prior to their due date.

Include administrative assistant in one client meeting each quarter.

Submit and discuss weekly meetings and schedules each Monday.

When conducting one-on-one meetings, do not allow interruptions (ever).

Schedule quarterly lunches to demonstrate appreciation.

Establish an "open-door, open-mind" policy that encourages honest discussion.

CROSSMARK Example 3: Service Action Plan for an Internal Group of Retail Representatives

CROSSMARK employs more than 14,000 full- and part-time in-store retail representatives. This large and effective field organization is managed by retail field supervisors, each of whom supervises an average of 30 retail representatives. This is a situation in which the scope of the constituency renders a group plan appropriate. Should there be individuals within the group with considerably different soft needs, separate Service Action Plans should be prepared for them. This third illustration is a Service Action Plan written by a CROSSMARK retail field supervisor for an internal constituency made up of retail representatives.

Who Is Being Served?
CROSSMARK retail representatives (constituency)

Soft Needs
To be respected

To be listened to, and heard

To be valued

To be recognized

To be informed

To be praised

To feel they are contributing

Service Actions
Return all e-mails and phone calls within 24 hours, even if only to update the retail representatives on the status of an outstanding issue.

Write a monthly newsletter recognizing outstanding team and individual achievements.

Provide honest and meaningful evaluation sessions each quarter.

Create an innovative team-building event to be held annually.

In every conversation with the retail representatives, recognize their accomplishments.

Copy the team on ideas, suggestions, and accomplishments that are forwarded "up the line."

For Whom Do I Create Service Action Plans?

Let's revisit our CROSSMARK account executives and administrative assistants for a moment. In our second CROSSMARK Service Action Plan example, we touched on the idea of service reciprocity. From there, it's an easy leap to the concept of service multiplicity, in which individuals serve numerous constituencies and individuals, many of whom overlap and many of whom are distinct. It's a complex web of relationships that in the realm of Service Excellence can move an organization forward or, lacking Service Excellence, can cause it to stumble.

Account Executives	*Administrative Assistants*
Serve	*Serve*
Clients	Clients
Administrative assistants	Account executives
Peer account executives	Peer administrative assistants
Company management	Company management
Retail support associates	Information technology
Internal marketing	Finance
Finance	Human resources
Human resources	

In contemplating this list and the complexities associated with so many relationships, it's reasonable to raise the question "Whom do I serve?" Simplistically, the answer could be "everyone." Realistically, the answer is "nearly everyone."

Let the 80/20 rule guide your creation of Service Action Plans. You should build individual Service Action Plans for those people who occupy 80 percent of your time. The remaining 20 percent are likely to be members of a department and, therefore, merit a Service Action Plan for constituents, as illustrated in our third CROSSMARK example.

Final Thoughts on Service Action Plans

Well-developed Service Action Plans are effective time management tools. Incorporate your service actions into your primary planning tools (Outlook, Franklin Covey, Day-Timer). If they are time bound and measurable, your action plans will logically become part of your daily, weekly, or monthly goals and tasks. This will also help ward off those time wasters that consume 16 hours of an average workweek.

Share your Service Action Plans with the other members of your team who serve the same individuals. Create or strengthen an environment of service that fosters equality; in collaboration lays the path to success. In the wise-beyond-his-years words of Mattie Stepanek in *Fortunes, Prayers, and Quotes*, "Unity is strength . . . when there is teamwork and collaboration, wonderful things can be achieved."

At first, creating Service Action Plans for your internal associates may feel awkward. It upends the flow of relationships inherent in hierarchical organizations. I overheard my son, Rob, likening this step of the process to learning to dance the tango:

> *When we began, the steps were uncomfortable and the result wasn't much fun to watch or be party to. Then we tried a new "service mojo" on others who were learning the dance. Sometimes we led and sometimes we followed. But patience with our partners, dedication to learning our steps, learning when to lead and when to follow, resulted in a tango that was both beautiful to watch and thrilling to dance.*

Monitor your service actions continuously to ensure that your quest to satisfy needs has not become monotonous or uninspired. Challenge yourself to be creative; it is one of the great traits of exceptional service people. Seek ingenuity in all that you do—including your meetings, voice-mails, e-mails, or your physical environment. Delight from the unexpected!

Don't just "work the plan"; *lead* those you serve. Remember, being a server is about doing the right thing. Always act in the best interests of those you serve. Gently demonstrate how your recommendations will result in the best outcome. In short, serve well through leadership.

A REALLY FUN LEARNING

Dan Sacco is, first, my friend and, second, my esteemed client at The Nielsen Company. One of my service actions is to make time for two social outings a year with Dan. In so doing, I plan to satisfy his soft needs to feel recognized, valued, and important.

Last summer, he and his wife Nancy were planning a week's vacation to Southern California. Seeking an opportunity to create memories, I invited them to a concert at the Hollywood Bowl. I happen to think "The Bowl" is one of Los Angeles's best entertainment venues, so I was thrilled when they accepted my invitation.

I immediately set about executing my plan. I visited the ticket office in person, and I inquired about whether any season ticket holders had released their enviable Garden or Terrace box seats for the concert we'd agreed to attend. I was delighted when the woman in the ticket office replied, "Actually several sets of box seats have been turned in for that date, so you have a few choices."

"More importantly," I responded, "before we select the seats, do you have any reserved valet parking passes for the concert? This is really essential."

You see, there is limited parking at The Bowl since this venue is literally built into the side of the Hollywood Hills. They employ a "stacked-parking" configuration for concerts, lining cars up bumper to bumper, side by side, denser than a dealer's lot. When a concert is over, you can't move until the car ahead of you does. But behind The Bowl's shell, next to the West Gate entrance, is valet parking. This lot, which requires a reservation, is always sold out since it facilitates a speedy exit.

Good fortune was shining upon me that day because there was just one valet parking pass to be had for the concert. I immediately snapped it up and then set about selecting our seats. "I really want to be in stage left—if you have any seats in that section, I'll take them!"

"Well, I do," she replied. "I can fulfill your request, but considering the importance you placed on valet parking, I think you will be better served by taking four other seats the same distance from the stage but on the opposite side of The Bowl at stage right."

"But that's not what I requested!"

She boldly proceeded, despite my doggedness about stage left: "The valet lot is located near stage right, and the exit to public parking is by stage left. At the end of the performance, if you're in stage left, you'll feel like a salmon swimming upstream as you work your way toward valet parking. By the time you reach the valet lot, the cars leaving public parking will be choking the valet exit lane."

I realized she was leading me to a better solution. "Do it!"

The concert was magnificent, the weather was perfect, and we had a delightful picnic on the grounds of The Bowl prior to the performance. At the conclusion of the concert, we quickly made our way to the car, exited the lot, and sailed past the public parking, which was at a complete standstill.

"Wow," Dan remarked, looking at the backup of cars, "they'll be there for a long time!"

LESSON TO REMEMBER

Had it not been for an attentive person at the box office, we might still be trying to exit the Hollywood Bowl. She understood my needs, listened to and heard me, and then led me to a better solution. In serving clients, the Service Action Plan is essential to satisfying soft needs. The quality of your plan will determine the outcome. People do not stumble upon Service Excellence; it is essential that you lead those you serve to this achievement.

9

Adopt the Traits of Great Service People

Service which is rendered without joy helps neither the servant nor the served. But all other pleasures and possessions pale into nothingness before service which is rendered in a spirit of joy.

—Mohandas Gandhi,
An Autobiography: The Story of My Experiments with Truth

Our roadmap to Service Excellence consists of five very tangible steps that, when followed, will result in higher levels of satisfaction for those you serve. But what separates good service people from exceptional service people, if not these steps? The answer is personal traits. This intangible aspect of Service Excellence is so important that we have devoted this entire chapter to characterizing the traits of great service people and demonstrating how they are fundamental to achieving a level of success that is remarkable.

How are *skill, behavior*, and *attitude* interrelated? As we recount the ventures of some well-known public figures, you will begin to appreciate how behavior and attitude define the very core of a person. It is not unusual for people to be admired, vilified, or simply remembered less for what they did (skill) than for *how* they did *what* they did (behavior and attitude).

As you embark upon this transformation process, you must be introspective about your own personal traits and take into consideration those of your colleagues. When you challenge people and organizations to act differently, success demands strength of character. Esteemed personal traits will see you through taxing times, so you need to assess the behaviors and attitudes of current and future team members. "Hire for attitude and train for skill" is a mantra of great service companies, but this can be accomplished only when you are able to recognize the personal traits that beget success.

Traits of Exceptional Service People

Regardless of the nature of your business, certain traits are common to all exceptional service people. Your culture is formed by a collection of people, so it follows that your goal must be to identify and draw on those who possess the desired traits. Only then can you effect your transformation to a culture of Service Excellence.

Understanding the traits of exceptional service people also facilitates the benchmarking of internal and external performance, the transfer of people across teams or companies, and the process for hiring new associates. So what are these traits?

Well, Gandhi's perspective is that "all other pleasures and possessions pale into nothingness before service which is rendered in a spirit of joy." Perhaps a slight overstatement, but the *desire to serve* is of paramount importance. If not present, serving others will be arduous, and your indifference, or possibly even contempt, cannot be disguised.

In addition to desire, we suggest that *humility* is closely associated with great service. *Webster's* defines *humility* as "being humble of mind and spirit, absent of arrogance and self-importance." Humility is the willingness to place the needs and desires of others above your own. Humble associates and leaders form humble organizations, from which great service is delivered. Humility is a fundamental trait of many of our benchmark service companies, including Southwest Airlines, Marriott, and Starbucks.

What Is the Difference between Behavior, Attitude, and Skill?

Behavior is how you act.
Attitude is a way of thinking.
Skill is the ability to do something well.

How often have you heard someone say, "It really doesn't matter how they behave. They are so good at what they do that their skills offset everything else."

Nothing could be further from the truth. You don't have to look long or hard to find examples of public figures with indisputable skills whose behaviors and attitudes have significantly impacted the individuals and organizations with whom they interact.

• Terrell Owens •

Remember a few years back when Terrell Owens was regarded by football fans as one of the best receivers to have played in the National Football League? In the 2004 to 2005 season, he was instrumental in leading the Philadelphia Eagles to the Super Bowl, only to lose to the New England Patriots by 3 points. But his volatile temper was a colossal distraction for the team, ultimately disrupting their chemistry. Half of his team members despised Owens; the other half supported him.

On November 2, 2005, ESPN quoted Eagles Coach Andy Reid as saying, "The tempestuous star receiver won't return to the Philadelphia Eagles this season—or probably ever—because of a large number of situations that have accumulated over a long period of time." Reid said the outspoken player had been warned repeatedly about the consequences of his actions. "We gave Terrell every opportunity to avoid this outcome."

Despite Owens's great skill, his dreadful behavior played a large role in his release from Philadelphia. No team can win without unity, and he single-handedly undermined the unison of the Eagles. Owens is now with the Dallas Cowboys, presumably trying to change his behavior as a result of the Philadelphia experience. Only time will tell.

• Barry Bonds •

While writing this book, Barry Bonds surpassed Henry Aaron as baseball's all-time home run leader. This was an achievement that should have been universally celebrated, but it was blemished by unresolved allegations of steroid use. Bonds' abysmal attitude in response to assertions of dishonest behavior will forever tarnish his record. After a series of events, including the public auction of the home run ball, the plan for the notorious ball was for it to be displayed in Cooperstown, imprinted with an asterisk in acknowledgment of the surrounding controversy. However, 2007 ended with Bonds' being indicted for lying to a grand jury about steroid use, so that chapter has yet to be closed.

• Tony Gwynn; Cal Ripken •

In stark contrast to Barry Bonds' career, the outstanding careers of Tony Gwynn and Cal Ripken were celebrated in the summer of 2007 when they were inducted into the Baseball Hall of Fame. If attendance is any indication of admiration, these great men were clearly revered by players and fans alike. The induction ceremony was attended by the largest-ever collection of living Hall of Famers (53), while a record 75,000 fans visited the baseball shrine that weekend. Both Gwynn and Ripken were consistently and broadly recognized for their professionalism, gracious demeanor, and respect for the game—in short, their behaviors and attitudes.

• 1980 USA Olympic Hockey Team •

For those who remember the 1980 Winter Olympics in Lake Placid, New York, the contrast in behaviors between the U.S. Hockey Team and Terrell Owens and Barry Bonds is stunning.

The 1980 Olympic Games were held during a time of pervasive diplomatic tension between the United States and the Soviet Union. The tension was palpable on the ice rink as well. The Soviet Olympic ice hockey team had medaled in every Winter Games tournament since 1960. They had been playing together for many years, though they lacked youth. In contrast, the American team was a collection of young college students with little history of playing together.

I came across this captivating article by Bruce Lowitt of the *St. Petersburg Times*, published December 26, 1999, nearly 20 years after the event:

> The Soviets were seeded No. 1, and deservedly so. They had won five gold medals and one bronze in the previous six Olympics. The U.S. team was seeded seventh.
>
> The U.S. and USSR teams each won their first five games. On Feb. 22, George Washington's birthday, patriotism was running rampant in and outside the Olympic Field House. The Soviets unleashed 30 shots in the first two periods to the United States' 10. Only one dramatic save after another by former Boston University goaltender Jim Craig kept the United States close.
>
> The Soviets led 3-2 after two periods. "We told ourselves we were just down one, when we'd been down six after two periods last time we played them," team member John Harrington said. "We'd played 40 minutes, they

were just one ahead, but we were younger. We wanted to take it to 'em." And take "'em" they did. The USA tied the game up, and then on a shot by Mike Eruzione, the team captain, took a 4-3 lead that held up for the victory.

As the final seconds counted down, broadcaster Al Michaels gained an immortality of sorts. "Do you believe in miracles?" he shouted, and at the final buzzer he answered, "Yes!"

Two days later, rallying from a 2-1 deficit, the U.S. team defeated Finland 4-2 to win the gold medal. Many remember where they were at the exact moment Team USA achieved this historic feat. I recall I was collecting my daughter, Susan, from her music lesson in Pearl River, New York. To this day, that victory with all its excitement and significance still ranks as one of my top sports memories.

Few fans or professional hockey analysts thought this young and inexperienced group of college kids could hold their own on the Olympic stage. Their skill was not near the level of other nations' teams. Few believed it . . . except for these young hockey players. What they lacked in skill, they more than compensated for in their positive attitude, behavior, desire, determination, and belief in one another. These traits won the gold medal for the United States that year.

• Martha Stewart •

Consider the contrast that is Martha Stewart, preprison versus postprison. Her disdain for the justice system was apparent as she was escorted out of a Manhattan courthouse following her conviction on four counts of obstructing justice and lying to investigators. For her crimes she was sentenced to six months in prison, a term that she fulfilled. The world-renowned "Diva of Domesticity," who had built an empire unlike any before her, found herself convicted of crimes that threatened to topple that very empire.

Her downfall was not a reflection of *what* she did (her job, or arguably even the well-timed stock trade). Her fall from grace was the result of *how* she did *what* she did (behavior and attitude). Guilty of avarice and arrogance, the justice system did not look kindly on her behavior in the wake of their investigation.

Back to the contrast that is Martha Stewart. Since her release from prison, she has indeed transformed *how* she does *what* she does. In so doing, she has restored her image and is now leading her conglomerate to even higher levels of success. This past summer, she happily announced to her viewing public, "Today ends my probation." Her punishment now a closed chapter, Martha Stewart is embarking on a personal transformation whose outcome has yet to be seen. We are encouraged by her journey thus far, as it substantiates our premise that by changing one's behaviors and attitudes, you can generate significantly different results.

Personal traits *do* impact our relationships and the perceptions of others. Let's continue to reinforce this premise.

• Martin Luther King; Oprah Winfrey •

Both Martin Luther King and Oprah Winfrey are recognized for their personal dedication to improving race relations in this country. King led a movement that challenged and transformed America's conscience on matters of racial equality. His passion, beliefs, attitudes, and behaviors forced a society to confront the rampant injustice of racism and effect change. King's famous "I Have a Dream" speech, delivered in August 1963, embodied his attitudes and sought to change a population's behaviors.

Were it not for the path forged by Martin Luther King, would Oprah Winfrey have been able to achieve her dreams? Regardless, she has used her fame, fortune, and media pulpit to right wrongs and change lives—all with grace, humor, and intellectual curiosity. In short, her attitudes and behaviors toward others will be her legacy.

• President Jimmy Carter •

History may judge Jimmy Carter's presidency harshly, but with the passage of time, he is more likely to be remembered for the selfless work he performs, most notably with Habitat for Humanity on behalf of the underemployed, and with diplomatic delegations on behalf of the United States. Always gracious and charitable, compassionate and generous, Jimmy Carter, above all, will be remembered for his behaviors and attitudes.

• Bill and Melinda Gates; Bono •

Recognized by *Time* magazine as the 2005 Persons of the Year, these individuals have used the fruits of their success (wealth and access) to wage battle against disease, poverty, and discrimination. While their skills have afforded them the means to be "Good Samaritans" (*Time* magazine's words), it is their attitudes and behaviors that have made them true humanitarians.

Whom do you respect and admire? Think of friends and relatives, personal heroes, celebrities, and other public figures—either living or deceased. What traits draw you to these people? Make a list, noting for each person the reasons he or she has earned your respect and admiration. We suspect the attitudes and behaviors will outweigh the skills on your list.

Traits of Our Benchmark Companies

Let us refer, once again, to our benchmark companies to illustrate our premise.

• Southwest Airlines •

Our experiences with Southwest have been consistent and delightful, in large part because of the service traits their culture practices and holds in high esteem:

- Humility and selflessness
- Sense of humor
- Going the extra mile
- Thinking like an owner to transcend functional boundaries
- Entrepreneurial spirit
- Responsible and proactive

• Marriott •

You could be in New York City, Des Moines, Paris, or Dubai, and you will observe the following behaviors and attitudes from Marriott's service people:

- Humility
- Well-cared-for associates, who mirror that care for their guests
- Valuing the organization over individual players
- Making fact-based decisions
- Visibly engaging in hands-on management
- Teamwork
- Attention to detail
- Believing "Success is never final"

• CROSSMARK •

During the final phase of CROSSMARK's transformation, we closely examined the concept of service traits. Soliciting the opinions of a large cross-section of associates, we sought to understand the traits they believed to be most important in serving well. How did they want their culture to evolve, and by what traits did they want to be defined?

We returned to our tried-and-true approach of brainstorming sessions. Thirty-five meetings and more than 100 traits later, we distilled the lists down to just 14 of the most commonly cited traits, all of which garnered support from across the organization:

Proactive behavior	Consistency
Creativity	Passion
Honesty	Loyalty
Integrity	Enthusiasm
Humility	Positive attitude
Respectfulness	Flexibility
Resourcefulness	Sense of humor

Of these 14 traits, 5 received consistently high rankings: proactive behavior, creativity, honesty, integrity, and humility. For illustrative purposes, we would like to delve into these first two traits for a more complete examination of the intrinsic role traits play in achieving Service Excellence.

Proactive Behavior

More than most traits, proactive behavior makes an almost immediate impact and generates visible results. When you observe proactive behavior, you know it. When you experience it, you feel it. When someone is proactive on your behalf, you are gratified. Clearly, this is an important trait in the pursuit of Service Excellence.

The definition of proactive behavior can be elusive, so I would like to share a great illustration of this trait in action. Last fall I was moderating a client advisory board meeting at the W Dallas Victory Hotel. Prior to the start of our meeting, I saw one of our board members, Kevin Mahon of Georgia Pacific, in the lobby. He appeared to be leaving the hotel, so I asked where he was going.

"I'm headed back to the airport. I grabbed the wrong luggage."

The W Hotel's alert concierge, Leslie Livingston (no relation), overheard our exchange and said, "Let us take care of that for you; it happens all the time."

Leslie located the owner's luggage ID tag and placed a call to the cell phone number on his business card. She was successful in reaching him and verified that he was the owner of the wayward bag. He was at another hotel about 30 minutes from the W, and Kevin's bag was still at the airport.

"Go to your meeting, Mr. Mahon," Leslie said. "We'll take care of this for you."

When Kevin returned to his room later that day, his lost bag was neatly placed on the luggage rack, with a note thanking him for staying at the W and informing him that both bags were with their rightful owners. *This is proactive behavior.* An attentive person overheard a problem, took ownership of the solution, and followed it through to a satisfactory conclusion.

The W Hotel trains their associates to be attentive to their surroundings and when they "listen and hear" any difficulty unfolding, to proactively take ownership of a solution and see it through. Leslie learned well.

How Do Proactive Behavior and Reactive Behavior Differ?

Proactive Behavior	*Reactive Behavior*
Goes the extra mile	Does only what's required
Exceeds expectations	Meets expectations
Takes calculated risks	Is risk averse
Thinks independently	Needs to be told
Anticipates problems	Solves problems
Seeks new solutions	Relies on status quo
Questions and challenges	Assumes
Is a multifunctional thinker	Does just the job
Sets goals	Operates from to-do lists

Roger Staubach, Hall of Fame quarterback and entrepreneur, had this observation: "There are no traffic jams along the extra mile." To build on this thought, you get a lot better mileage from proactive behavior because your client's satisfaction from the experience lingers well beyond the event.

Creativity

"Do the common thing in an uncommon way!" In a service relationship, which typically involves any number of customary transactions, you run the risk of stagnating. By bringing your imagination to the relationship, you create excitement and growth.

Creativity is new ideas. Creativity untethers your thoughts. Your individual creativity, combined with relevant service actions, can produce unique and stimulating outcomes. Your imagination fuels your creativity, and creativity is the key to great service.

Let's head back to Dallas and the W Hotel for an example of how creativity can turn a routine activity into a memorable experience. I can't begin to estimate the number of meetings in drab hotel conference rooms I've attended over the course of my career. But I can tell you what almost every single meeting room looked like: white or beige table cloths draped over folding tables, cloudy glasses beside pitchers of water, plain note pads with the hotel logo, ball point pens, and hard candies your children would have rejected from their Halloween stash.

When I entered the W meeting room, I was astonished by their creative set-up. The tables were wrapped in black spandex and adorned with bold colors. There were the requisite memo pads with logos, but all the pencils bore clever phrases like "WHEN you want to write," "WHATCHA Thinking? Write it down!" and "WHY not write that down?" Glass carafes with four different kinds of fruit-flavored water, as well as high-end brands of bottled water, complemented the colorful meeting snacks of green apples and Starburst candies. The coasters for our glasses were as witty as the pencils; I collected three to take with me, each with a different message:

WHAT YOU THINK IS IMPORTANT! (Speak your mind.)

WHAT IS THE BIG PICTURE? (Close your eyes and see it.)

WHAT ARE YOU THINKING RIGHT AT THIS VERY SECOND? (Write it down.)

Other interesting items placed at each table delighted our meeting attendees:

- A fan (to stay cool in the Dallas heat, but as we discovered, also ideal for opinion voting)
- A small purple "tangle" toy (to occupy your hands and relieve stress; check them out at www.tangletoy.com)
- A decision pin wheel (to spin for advice on how to vote)
- An hour glass (to use as an impartial time tracker)

Brett Briseno, the W's convention services manager in Dallas, shared with me their approach to the meeting room experience. "We call our setup the 'sensory set,' which is created to please all five senses. In addition to the visual, tactile, and savory items, we pipe in music that meeting leaders can turn on or off at will. Before the start of a meeting and during breaks, we spray the room with a specially developed scent, exclusive to the W. We also encourage our meeting room staff to add their own touches, so every W meeting experience is unique."

How creative! Using their imagination, the W has done the common in an uncommon way; they have created excitement in an otherwise routine event. By letting your imagination fuel your creativity, you will enrich the service experience.

Seek Opportunities to Create Memories

How Can I Be Different?

You must consistently challenge yourself to be different. But how do you train your imagination to be the tool of your creative process? How can you discipline yourself to remove the boundaries you've placed on your mind? How can you eliminate your reluctance to do something different? How do you force yourself out of your comfort zone and take risks?

Answer these questions and your "creativity potion" will improve appreciably. Constantly ask yourself, "How can I be different?"

How Can I Stand Out?

In our increasingly technological world, differentiating yourself can be as simple as making personal connections with those you serve. The following suggestions, so rudimentary we're somewhat embarrassed to list them, will raise you above the rank and file:

- *Send handwritten thank you, acknowledgment, and appreciation notes.* Few people bother to do this anymore; when was the last time you received one? A colleague of mine, with nearly 2 million flight miles on United Airlines, received this handwritten note from Captain Gary Bjorklund on one of her flights: "I would like to THANK YOU for all the flying you do with us. We do appreciate your business!" She still has that note.
- *Personalize your voice-mail greeting.* When was the last time you changed your spiel? "I'm either away from my desk or on another call. Your call is very important to me . . ." Really? Let people know where you are, an alternate number where you can be reached, or the person's name and number who can provide immediate assistance. Mix it up; use your imagination; reflect your personality in your greeting.

- *Celebrate the important milestones in others' lives—births, birthdays, weddings, anniversaries, and special occasions.* Every planning tool tracks these events, so you're not even required to have a particularly good memory. Surprise those you serve by acknowledging their achievements. But don't limit yourself to life's celebratory events. Put your discomfort aside, and acknowledge the more poignant moments when those you serve encounter adversity. Stand out.

- *Judiciously use the vast resources of the Internet to forward items of interest to those you serve.* Don't pass on jokes or links to sites that interest *you*—you will stand out, but not in the manner you'd hoped. When you know and understand a person's needs, technology—used wisely—can be a differentiator.

- *Schedule time with your clients, preferably away from the office, to brainstorm ways in which you can improve your relationship.* Guard against conversations regarding the work you perform on their behalf (*what* you do); the time should be devoted to the service component of your relationship (*how* you do *what* you do). Imagine how infrequent these kinds of discussions are in your world, and you can imagine the extent to which this will differentiate you.

Brainstorming

Brainstorming is a powerful tool that, unfortunately, tends to gather rust in our tool sheds. It is an effective means for generating new ways in which to create memorable experiences for those you serve. But it is also an art, as evidenced by the number of experts who specialize in this discipline.

In the absence of an expert, how do you get started? Ask open-ended questions, such as "What if . . . ?" "Suppose I . . . ?" "How can I . . . ?" Put yourself in the other person's shoes. What would make them say "Wow"? Pretend you're planning a surprise party. How do you ensure the party remains a surprise? After the first 30 seconds of the party, how will you continue to surprise and delight?

Ask yourself these three questions:

1. What can I do that they won't experience elsewhere?
2. What can I do that is totally unexpected?
3. Will this action create a good memory?

When brainstorming with a group of people, adhere to these simple rules:

- No "devil's advocate."
- No criticisms, because . . .
- There are no bad ideas.
- Keep presenting ideas.
- Everyone speaks once before someone speaks twice, to ensure . . .
- Everyone participates and contributes.
- Stay focused on your goal.

The following story illustrates the power of creative brainstorming and the remarkable results that can come from this activity.

Dabney Bixel is the creative and energetic owner of Bixel & Company, an event planning firm in Southern California. General Motors was organizing a large dealer incentive meeting, focusing on Beverly Hills as a venue thanks to the efforts of many of Dabney's local competitors. Unfortunately, the GM meeting planners had been underwhelmed by the sales presentations of these competitive firms, and they had decided to strike Beverly Hills from consideration.

Because of this decision, the GM meeting planners had opted to cut short their Los Angeles inspection. This meant canceling the previously scheduled meeting with Dabney and the Beverly Wilshire hotel. Unwilling to concede defeat, particularly since they hadn't even had the opportunity to step up to the plate, Dabney and her hotel contacts met to brainstorm creative ideas for salvaging this potentially large engagement. Unable to resist Dabney's powers of persuasion, GM eventually agreed to reschedule the meeting with her but with strict parameters. They would meet her in the lobby bar of the Beverly Wilshire hotel and allow only 30 minutes for her pitch.

At exactly 6 p.m., Dabney met the General Motors executives in the lobby bar. She began by describing her idea for an event that would be held across from the hotel at the posh address of Two Rodeo Drive. Her plan was to hold a special catered dinner—on the street itself—of this famous drive.

At 6:15 p.m., as planned in their brainstorming session, Wolfgang Puck appeared at the table carrying two boxes of his signature pizzas. He pulled up a chair and, in his rich Austrian accent, said to the GM people, "What is this I'm told you are not coming to LA to have me cook for your people on Rodeo Drive? Can they do that elsewhere?"

Once the surprise of Wolfgang's appearance had subsided and the pizza and champagne were consumed, GM agreed to reopen the idea of hosting their dealer incentive meeting in Beverly Hills. And, eventually, Dabney and her firm triumphed; the business was theirs. *Creativity*, fostered by brainstorming, won the day. What appeared to be a hopeless situation was, in fact, an opportunity to create memories.

We have touched on the many traits that separate good from exceptional service people and characterize Service Excellence. The question you must ask yourself is, what traits do you want to epitomize you and your culture? You must answer this question before embarking on your transformation. Those traits will define you and your company, guide the development of your new culture, help identify the people who will contribute to your momentum (and those who will not), and shape your hiring practices. The importance of this intangible aspect of Service Excellence simply cannot be emphasized enough.

Again, *how* you do *what* you do will determine who you will become.

LEARNING FROM A LEGEND

I graduated from St. John's University in Jamaica, Queens. During my enrollment, we were privileged to have Joe Lapchick as our basketball coach, a sports figure of great character. Gus Alfieri, a classmate and member of the basketball team, has written an outstanding book about his coach entitled *Lapchick: The Life of a Legendary Player and Coach in the Glory Days of Basketball.*

Coach Lapchick, a man of great integrity, honor, and humility, was a pioneer in the game of basketball. He played for the original Celtics, was the first coach of the New York Knickerbockers, and helped promote integration in the NBA by coaching the first African-American player in the league.

Last summer, I was privileged to have dinner with Gus and some of his friends: Jack Kaiser, former director of athletics at St. John's, and Lou Carnesecca, Joe Lapchick's assistant coach and ultimate replacement when Joe retired from coaching. It was a great night of reminiscing about St. John's basketball and Coach Lapchick.

Lou began sharing stories about his mentor, recalling a particularly memorable exchange early in his coaching career. For whatever reason, Coach Lapchick felt his protégé was paying too much attention to the recent spate of flattering press clippings. So Joe handed Lou a small piece of paper and said, "Read this whenever you think you're getting too good." With this, Lou reached into his wallet and retrieved the well-worn piece of paper Coach Lapchick had given him nearly 50 years ago. It read:

Peacock today; feather duster tomorrow.

"I carry it with me to this day," confessed Coach Carnesecca.

LESSON TO REMEMBER

If we had to pick but one trait as an unconditional requirement for everyone in a service business, it would be humility. Only through humility can we achieve greatness in our relationships with those we serve. Without humility, feather dusters are our destiny.

3

The New Beginning

10

Seek Continuous Improvement

Without continual growth and progress, such words as improvement,
achievement, and success have no meaning.

—Benjamin Franklin

The pursuit of Service Excellence is not a destination; it is
a journey. You do not attain Service Excellence, check the
box, and move on to the next initiative. Before embarking on
your Service Excellence transformation, you must be prepared to
commence what, in essence, will be the perpetual pursuit of ever-
higher levels of satisfaction and of *seeking better ways to be better*.
When you improve how you serve others, you raise the bar; what
was once exceptional service is now the norm. If this seems daunting,
take heart; cultures that champion continuous improvement foster
creativity, imagination, innovation, and self-examination.

What Can We Learn from the Past?

When you hear the maxim "continuous improvement," you're
likely to call to mind the Total Quality Management (TQM) pan-
acea of the 1980s and 1990s. "Quality Improvement" became a
universally chanted corporate mantra, but remarkably, these im-

provement initiatives focused solely on the *what*, and rarely on the *how*.

- "Quality" equated to process improvement, which then defined company objectives: zero defects, waste elimination, work flow efficiencies.
- Quality Improvement teams proliferated. Graphs, charts, signs, and slogans filled offices, cubes, conference rooms, and cafeterias. Processes and work flows were diagrammed in infinitesimal detail.

What was the result? Processes improved, margins grew, and cost savings were tabulated and heralded with the fervor of a televangelist. More meetings were scheduled to root out waste, more work flows were diagrammed and analyzed, and no person or department escaped scrutiny. "Better, faster, cheaper" became the Holy Grail. But then something insidious began to happen. In an attempt to streamline and simplify, companies began to overthink and overcomplicate their processes, creating a new brand of waste. I still consider this one of the most careless eras of contradiction ever encountered in my career.

Public acknowledgment of one's quality became the highly coveted brass ring to which all CEOs aspired. One of the most widely recognized of these accolades is the Malcolm Baldrige National Quality Award. This program, inspired by the precepts of TQM, rewards quality in the business, health-care, education, and nonprofit sectors. Its purpose is to enhance U.S. competitiveness by helping improve organizational performance practices, facilitating cross-sector sharing of best practices, and providing tools for planning, managing, and learning.

Today's process improvement programs have evolved from the early days of TQM to become more streamlined and sophisticated. Six Sigma, the program created by Motorola and popularized by General Electric, interjected some common sense into the process improvement movement. Kaizen and Lean are other highly regarded adaptations of that quality process. But all of these programs still have one disturbing thing in common: they are primarily about the *what*!

Why is this disturbing? We believe the TQM-inspired movement inadvertently contributed to the decay of relationships between companies and their clients. These programs required a laser focus on internal processes and the work itself, distracting people and organizations from those they served. Entire companies became consumed by *what* they did, leaving their client relationships to wither from neglect.

This neglect was further exacerbated by the technological "quality solutions" that ushered in our era of personal detachment. As an outcome of the quest for "better, faster, cheaper," customers were forced to interact with computers first and, if they lucked out, humans second. So the question is: Are we serving clients better as a result of our focus on the *what*? Have we improved the customer experience?

The answer is *No!*

But imagine, for a moment, the impact on your company and clients if you were to expend the same degree of energy, thought, and creativity to improving relationships with those you serve. In concert with your process improvements, what would happen to your relationships and customer loyalty if your entire company focused on improving value for your clients? What would be the impact of simultaneously improving the *what and* the *how*? What if those charts on the walls of your workplace declared the needs, service actions, and creative behaviors required to add value to your services and/or products for your clients? What a compelling opportunity!

This chapter discusses the simple practices that are essential for continuously improving the service you provide: setting perceptions aside and discerning reality, getting feedback, innovating, and delivering value. These are truly uncomplicated practices, which is the reason we opened this chapter by reviewing past improvement initiatives; you must guard against overengineering these steps and being doomed to repeat history. We will conclude our discussion with the topic of celebrating your successes, as that is what motivates people to keep searching for *better ways to be better*.

Perception versus Reality

Bain & Company surveyed the senior executives at 362 firms across several industries to quantify the gap between perception and reality in the realm of Service Excellence. The results were startling:

- 80 percent of those companies providing services believed they *delivered* "*superior* service and experiences" to their clients.
- Among those same clients, only 8 percent felt they *received* "*superior* service and experiences."

In the best-case scenario (a complete overlap of the 8 percent and 80 percent), 9 out of 10 service providers think they're doing a better job than those on the receiving end. This disconnect is at best, frustrating; at worst, the precursor to a severed relationship. Unfortunately, the following sentiment is not as uncommon as you might think: "*I'm shocked the client fired us! I thought our relationship was great and that I was doing a really good job.*"

So how do you bring perception and reality into alignment? Talk frequently. Ask questions. Probe the answers. Never assume. Recognize soft needs. And get feedback!

Get Feedback

Continual improvement is an unending journey.

—Lloyd Dobyns and Clare Crawford-Mason,
Thinking About Quality

In matters of service, ignorance is absolutely not bliss. The absence of any direct or specific feedback can allow one to believe their clients are well served (*"they'd say something if they were upset"*). Without adequate information you may assume the relationship is healthy. When you confuse your perceptions with your clients' reality, you walk away from opportunities to increase your clients' satisfaction—or worse, allow yourself to become vulnerable.

A common misstep is the way in which people behave when relationships are in a state of calm. When everything is working as it should, it is human nature to shift your attention elsewhere and put the client relationship on cruise control. You assume all is well, you relax, and complacency sets in. This lapse has potentially devastating consequences.

A better approach is to view this calm as the perfect time to proactively focus on the client relationship. Think about it. When *what* you do is working well, people are happy, their demands are less thorny, tensions abate, time is more plentiful, communications flow more freely, and life is good. Sound performance opens doors. Use this opportunity to gather feedback, develop a genuine understanding of your clients' soft needs, and focus on building that coveted bridge to loyalty.

The perfect time to solicit client feedback is during periods of outstanding performance, but not for the reasons you may think. When *what* you do is on track, you can probe for feedback on your *behaviors* without any distractions from product performance issues. Great service companies use feedback mechanisms that ask for input when their clients are the most satisfied. This approach takes advantage of the client relationship at its high points, resulting in commentary about the most important aspect of the relationship: behaviors. It also conveys your quest for continuous improvement, which registers with clients and gives rise to more open and willing participation.

- After purchasing a new automobile, the great service companies ask about your buying experience.

- After visiting a quality hotel, they ask for feedback about your stay.
- After shopping at a fine department store, they ask about your interactions with their sales associates.

Great service companies solicit feedback using some form of personal connection, such as telephone calls. Be careful not to undermine the very objective you are trying to achieve by asking those you serve to engage in annoying and impersonal feedback mechanisms. Think about interactive voice surveys, comment cards, suggestion boxes, or e-mail surveys. Reflect on your personal experiences with airlines, Internet service providers, and online retailers who routinely ask you to participate in surveys lasting longer than the transaction. These mechanisms may be cheaper and faster, but are they really better? What is the quality of the feedback?

Use Surveys

Used properly, surveys that solicit feedback from internal and external clients can be very effective. But your intentions must be pure or the process can backfire. Are you really seeking continuous improvement, or are you eliciting praise? Your clients are not easily duped; they can see through self-congratulatory mechanisms that, as an aside, typically miss the mark.

Requests for feedback must be ongoing, timely, specific, easy to complete, and limited to vital indicators of satisfaction. Your goal is to ascertain areas requiring improvement and the extent to which the improvement would enhance client satisfaction. Needs that have been satisfied, while gratifying, are not really motivators. If you are well intentioned about seeking continuous improvement, you must be inspired by what you are missing, not by the targets you hit. Properly designed surveys will lead you to these answers.

Thoughts on Surveys

The following are some thoughts on surveying internal and external clients. Vary your survey methods, and you will assemble more robust and multidimensional information from which to develop continuous improvement plans. And remember, you are seeking areas of improvement, not affirming your beliefs. Some techniques include the following:

- *Mystery callers and mystery shoppers.* These techniques are effective when used as training vehicles, not as fodder for reprimands.
- *Service advisory boards.* Populated by clients, the interactive nature of these vehicles results in a deeper understanding of the relationship.
- *Client service review meetings.* These interactions are most effective when held frequently and regularly because they create open forums to focus on clients' soft needs.
- *Web-enabled client surveys.* Albeit impersonal vehicles, surveys conducted this way encourage timely input and participation from those who may not otherwise speak up.

Surveying External Clients

At the start of your cultural transformation, engage the services of an independent third party to survey your external clients:

- Take advantage of the third party's expertise to develop survey questions that will get to the heart of your clients' soft needs.
- Establish a baseline from which your improvement can be measured.

- Broadly publish your survey results as a means of including, informing, and categorically demonstrating your desire for continuous improvement.
- Include Service Excellence metrics in all top-to-top client meetings.

Surveying Internal Clients

Engage the services of an independent third party to survey your internal clients as well. In order to obtain honest feedback on the "state of service" from your internal associates, you must guarantee anonymity to dispel fears of retribution.

Probe on topics such as these:

- The extent to which the culture/company/team/ manager engenders trust, honesty, respect, integrity, and communication
- Perceptions regarding opportunities for advancement
- Managerial and mentoring skills of direct managers
- Attentiveness and involvement of senior management
- Eagerness to recommend the company as a place to work
- Characterization of role: advocate, cheerleader, hostage, unindicted coconspirator or, God forbid, enemy combatant?

Internal Service Evaluations

Unfortunately, 360-degree reviews seem to run neck in neck with public speaking and death as people's greatest fears. This powerful, albeit slightly unnerving, practice is fundamental to an open culture of continuous improvement. However, if you are to effect a true cultural transformation, you must get past your discomfort and implement 360-degree practices:

- Build a nonthreatening mechanism for 360-degree feedback.
- Train associates on appropriate ways to give and receive feedback.
- Nurture an environment in which peer assessment is valued and welcomed.
- Closely observe the behavioral traits of colleagues.
- Do not allow "sacred cows" (for example, senior management).
- Reward positive suggestions for service improvement.

Feedback is really your only means of distinguishing perception from reality and is at the very core of a culture of continuous improvement. As with any discipline, soliciting feedback can be detailed and cumbersome or simple and practical. We vote for the latter.

"Seek and Ye Shall Find"

It is not complicated. Ask the person you serve two very simple and straightforward questions:

1. **I want to make sure my interactions with you meet, or better, exceed your expectations. So please tell me three aspects you like most about my approach to serving you.**
2. **Also, please tell me three things I need to do better in order to improve my approach to serving you.**

I promise you that the first time you ask these questions, your client will likely appear dazed, nervous, suspicious, or confused. Why? It is because clients are rarely, if ever, asked these questions by the people who serve them. They will be taken aback. But their initial discomfort will ease, and your reward will be a wealth of invaluable information about your service relationship.

In general, people are much more comfortable delivering good news, so you can expect your client to reply by listing all of your positive attributes. This is beneficial for two reasons. First, it is an easier conversation to have, and the more your clients enjoy the process, the more likely they are to welcome future exchanges. Second, and this is for you, if a client can't think of three positives, or the three cited are picayune (*"the color of your letterhead is pleasing to the eye"*), that in itself is a potent message.

However, because this is about continuous *improvement*, the more important feedback is what your clients ask you to do better. At first, this will likely feel awkward and embarrassing. But remember, by virtue of having this conversation, you are satisfying many of your clients' soft needs (to feel important, listened to, and respected) and validating the importance of your relationships.

What if a client insists there are no improvements to be made? Since there is little likelihood that everyone you serve is 100 percent satisfied, this answer means you will have to rely on others or a keen capacity for self-assessment to find areas of improvement. After all, if there is nothing you can do better, how will you grow the relationship?

Never have this "conversation" via e-mail or voice-mail. You must ask these questions in person, make eye contact, observe body language, read emotions, and factor in the surroundings. Have a *conversation*. If your clients are hesitant to talk, gently probe, revisit some successes, check to see if they would prefer a different time or place. But most of all, *talk often* because it will get easier and more fruitful with time and practice.

How Do You Deal with Feedback?

Defense attorneys assert that "you should never ask a question of a witness on the stand if you don't already know the answer."

Perhaps a bit dramatic for our purposes, but it speaks to the value of preparation. Do not seek feedback from your clients until you have thought about your questions, the clients' potential responses, and your subsequent reactions. Your conversations can be productive only if you don't overreact or get defensive, and the remedy for that is preparation. Think through these questions:

1. How will my clients react to my questions?
2. How will I feel about their responses?
3. Will I immediately become defensive, and why?
4. Will I believe what they say, and why?
5. Do I plan to take action regarding their responses?

This last point is important. Feedback given but not acknowledged in the form of action is little more than idle conversation. Recall our discussion regarding time management? Taking specific and visible actions based on your clients' feedback will guard against these interactions contributing to that disturbing number of 16 unproductive hours in a 45-hour workweek.

Innovation and Great Service

> Unless you try to do something beyond what you have already mastered, you will never grow.
>
> —Ralph Waldo Emerson

When feedback is established as one of the underpinnings of client relationships, it opens lines of communication and fosters dialogue. Expertly executed, the frequency of your interactions will increase, you will become well versed in the clients' business, your role will shift from supplier to trusted advisor, and you will be in a position to make informed contributions to their growth plans. Partnering this way stimulates creativity and shrewd innovation in both service and product design. What follows are some well-known companies who beautifully illustrate this process.

• Apple •

Steven Jobs views innovation this way: "You can't just ask customers what they want and then try to give that to them. By the time you get it built, they'll want something new." How true, particularly in this era of fleeting fads and short attention spans. Apple's iPods have evolved significantly in look, feel, and capability since their introduction. By seeking feedback from their users and listening to and hearing their soft needs, Apple has continuously (and sometimes imperceptibly) improved the iPod. As of summer 2007, consumers had downloaded 3 billion songs—proof that Apple has transformed how people listen to music and how they purchase it, and in the process, they have reshaped the music industry.

Apple is very much in touch with consumers and their imaginations. You need look no further than an Apple Store to see the connection or the new iPhone to experience the creativity. Their products satisfy consumers' hard technology needs, but their innovation is driven by a strong connection to people's soft needs (to be leading edge, cool, stylish, trendy, sophisticated) established through continuous feedback and dialogue.

• Target •

Have you filled a prescription at Target recently? Their redesigned prescription bottles sit upside down, are color coded for different family members, have large-print labels, and have a slot to hold drug interaction information. Bottles for liquids get a receptacle for oral syringes. These commonsense innovations—the first in 40 years—came about because Target listened to the feedback from Deborah Adler, a consumer who brought her ideas to Target after her grandmother mistakenly took her grandfather's prescription medication.

Presented with Ms. Adler's ideas, Target ran with the concept, asking her to serve as a consultant to their design team. Pharmacists, consumers, and engineers all contributed to transforming the ordinary into the extraordinary. Paying close attention to the soft needs of their prescription drug users, Target's innovation satisfied people's needs to feel safe, assured, and in control.

• 3M •

3M has been recognized as one of this country's most innovative companies. Their formula for innovation: "New ideas—plus action or implementation—which result in an improvement, a gain or a profit." Consider the ubiquitous Post-it notes. Through creativity, imagination, and a strong connection with their consumers, 3M's disappointment in a new type of glue's ability to adhere became an innovation that has transformed how we communicate with one another and organize ourselves.

Unfortunately, 3M's reputation as an innovator has been sliding in recent years. In 2004, 3M was ranked No. 1 on Boston Consulting Group's Most Innovative Companies list (now the *BusinessWeek/* BCG list). They dropped to No. 2 in 2005, No. 3 in 2006, and No. 7 in 2007. Why the decline? Think back to our discussion about quality improvement programs, their propensity for overcomplication, and their tendency to distract companies from client relationships.

Dev Patnaik, managing associate of innovation for Jump Associates, has this observation about 3M: "People have kind of forgotten about these guys. When was the last time you saw something innovative or experimental coming out of there? It's not uncommon for Six Sigma to become an end unto itself. That may be appropriate in an operations context—at the end of the year it's easy enough for a line manager to count up all the money he's saved by doing green-belt projects. But what 3Mers came to realize is that these financially definitive outcomes were much more elusive in the context of a research lab." Adds Larry Wendling, staff vice president of 3M's Corporate Research Laboratory, "In some cases in the lab [Six Sigma] made sense, but in other cases, people were going around dreaming up green-belt programs to fill their quota of green-belt programs for that time period. We were letting, I think, the process get in the way of doing the actual invention."

Benchmark Companies and Innovation

There are many great examples of innovation borne of a company's connection to their consumers, an unending quest for feedback, and commitment to a culture of continuous improvement. *BusinessWeek* recognizes the best-in-class companies in their annual Most Innovative Companies list (2007 rankings noted below). Reflect on these top 20 innovators, and think about your personal connections with these companies. The common threads are their service centricity and unblinking focus on their client relationships. Incidentally, you will note that these organizations all have enviable balance sheets:

1. Apple
2. Google
3. Toyota
4. GE
5. Microsoft
6. Procter & Gamble
7. 3M
8. Disney
9. IBM
10. Sony

11. Wal-Mart
12. Honda
13. Nokia
14. Starbucks
15. Target
16. BMW
17. Samsung
18. Virgin
19. Intel
20. Amazon[1]

Deliver Value

For the past 15 years, I have had the privilege of working with The Nielsen Company, the world's leading provider of marketing information, audience measurement, and business media products and services. Dan Sacco is the senior vice president of the client service organization for Nielsen's marketing information group.

Upon assuming this leadership position, Dan proposed that the measure of Nielsen's success should be the extent to which clients perceive they are receiving value, as opposed to a self-assessment of internally focused metrics. He immediately changed the client service incentive structure from one based on sales targets to one based on how they serve clients and add value to their relationships. This is measured using the *Value Management Objective* (VMO) process, in which performance criteria are set and evaluated by the clients themselves. In Dan's words, "To succeed, we must ask the client, 'What are the business issues you are trying to address? Is our work important? Are we doing a good job? Are we creating value for your company?' And we must ask these questions every single day."

---

1 Source: bwnt.businessweek.com/interactive_reports/most_innovative/index.asp?chan=innovation_special+report+---+2007+most+innovative+companies_2007+most+innovative+companies.

Implementing the VMO process has taken time and effort, but it is now ingrained in Nielsen's client service culture. To appreciate just how thoroughly this process observes the simple conventions of continuous improvement, let's examine its management of perception versus reality, feedback, and innovation.

The best way to align your perceptions with the client's reality is by reaching agreement on the priorities, actions, and outcomes of your service relationship. VMO is a disciplined process that begins with discussions about the client's business issues and priorities. Then, both parties agree on the insights and solutions that Nielsen will deliver in response to those priorities, and they will establish how Nielsen's contributions to create value will be measured by the client. VMO grounds the relationship in explicit, tangible, predictable, and reciprocal actions and evaluations, which is the recipe for significantly narrowing any gap between perception and reality.

Once the VMO work plan is established, the actual work commences. This is the time for vigorous feedback since it requires the joint assessment of analytic approaches, client input to monitor impact, problem resolution, course correction, and the capturing of opportunities that will create value. The importance of Nielsen's amended incentive structure comes into play here. Freed from pressures that may have resulted in redundant sales to clients, the organization can focus almost exclusively on delivering value. This shift in the drivers of compensation, combined with the intrinsic feedback component of the VMO process, changes the nature of the service relationship; clients begin to use the words *trusted*, *partner*, and *advisor* when describing Nielsen.

As Nielsen's client service teams immerse themselves in their clients' businesses and align their servicing with clients' priorities, they capture a wealth of information. Working to solve complex, and sometimes intractable, business issues challenges Nielsen and clients alike to bring their knowledge and ideas to the table. These experiences build trust, stimulate creativity, and fuel innovation.

The principles for continuous improvement are all found within the discipline of VMO. And then there's the "cherry on top" called *Value Creation*. Nielsen knows this program has successfully delivered value to their clients because clients have told them so. The service teams know they're aligned with clients, working on the right priorities, contributing to their successes, and adding value because their clients have confirmed, quantified, and endorsed the results.

Success begets success, and by virtue of the value created from the VMO process, doors have opened for Nielsen, exposure to senior levels of their clients has increased, their opportunities for value-added analyses have surged, resources have been redeployed to areas where they can deliver the greatest value, price discussions have transformed into value discussions, and so it continues.

Finally, one of the great hallmarks of The Nielsen Company is the willingness of everyone, regardless of assignment, to do whatever it takes to deliver value to clients. In the words of John Lewis, their North American CEO, "Everybody has to play their role, but everybody must do their part to support the team. It is important that clients hear 'one voice' that in effect serves as a chorus formed by the team." Ultimately, it is this genuine commitment to teamwork that enables an entire organization to stand and deliver value.

And Then, Celebrate Your Success

> The toughest thing about success is that you've got to keep on being a success.
>
> —Irving Berlin

Celebrating your success is important. Celebrations nourish the spirit, reward perseverance, recognize contributions, and motivate people to excel. They remind people that accomplishments are important, exciting, and worth celebrating. Celebrations can also present joyful opportunities to reinforce goals and recommunicate priorities.

There are many reasons to celebrate. Marking the end of a major project, winning a piece of business, or reaching an important milestone—these are all cause for celebration.

Be inclusive and be sure everyone shares in the festivities. Although everyone has a different role, we are hard pressed to think of successes that haven't come to fruition by the efforts of a team. Recognize the contributions of managers, peers, subordinates, and support staff; senior management, board members, and advisors; and clients and suppliers. All are part of your success.

Final Thoughts on Continuous Improvement

It is an indisputable fact that when you serve others, there will be times when your clients or customers will get angry or upset. They have high expectations and can try your patience, but you must listen, hear, solve, respond, and strive always to exceed their expectations. If you succeed, they will show their gratitude with more business and maybe even by expressing their appreciation. Remember that your clients' ultimate satisfaction will determine your ultimate success.

We leave you with this thought: If you want to practice continuous improvement from a personal perspective, we encourage you to do *one* extraordinary thing for *one* person *every* single day. We hope it will become a habit for you and an inspiration for others:

- Perform one unexpected act of service.
- Make one complimentary remark.
- Create one service memory.

- Say one kind word about another person.
- Do one thing that is "not your job."
- Reach out to someone you haven't spoken to in a long time.
- Perform one act of charity on behalf of someone in need.

Do not bother just to be better than your contemporaries or predecessors. Try to be better than yourself.

—William Faulkner

A LYRICAL LEARNING

It was late September 2001. I was sitting on a sparsely populated plane, anxiously awaiting take-off on my first flight since 9/11. I was apprehensive when the flight attendant escorted a young man up to first class and offered him the empty seat next to mine. In those jittery days following 9/11, people were hypersensitive to their seatmates.

We struck up a conversation, in part to ease the anxiety. I began by interrogating him about his seat change, and he reluctantly admitted that the flight attendant knew his work.

"Oh, what do you do?" I asked.

"I'm an artist."

Practicing my probing skills, I followed with more questions. "What kind of artist are you? Do you paint?"

"No, I'm a country music artist. My name is Brad Paisley."

We continued our conversation for the duration of our flight from Burbank to Dallas. Upon landing, we exchanged phone numbers, bid each other good-bye, and like most on-board encounters, never expected to hear from one another again.

But this bright young man had made an impression on me; he seemed wiser than his years as he discussed his career and the path he envisioned for himself. So out of curiosity, I logged on to his Web site and learned that Brad was in his late twenties, had just released his second CD, and was in the early stages of an exciting career. In 2000, he had been honored with the Country Music Association's (CMA) Horizon Award for the most promising new performer.

About a month later, we had the occasion to meet again. We began a nice relationship, talking about family, careers, career growth, professional improvement, and moving to the "next level." Around this same time, Brad was introduced to a delightful young woman, Kimberly Williams, best known for her roles in the *Father of the Bride* films and as Dana on the long-running television show *According to Jim*.

Kim lived in Santa Monica, so during their courtship Brad spent a fair amount of time in Southern California. We would get together from time to time and talk about different aspects of his career. Brad had dreams of being sponsored by a major company, so I scheduled meetings with the senior executives at some of my clients to discuss the responsibilities that an artist has to a sponsor. We visited Nestlé and Dole in Southern California, Unilever at Wal-Mart's headquarters in Bentonville, Arkansas, and J. Walter Thompson, an advertising agency in New York City.

By 2002, Brad had two No. 1 Billboard country singles, but he dreamed of having more (he now has 12 to his credit). He was the opening act for many of country music's biggest headliners, but he dreamed of headlining his own tour one day. What set Brad apart from so many, though, is that he didn't just dream. Brad worked extraordinarily hard at continuing to improve in all aspects of his career. He worked diligently on his song writing, guitar playing, video creations, and concerts. He experimented with performing different kinds of songs to expand his fan base. Brad didn't leave his career for others to decide; he took ownership for his own growth and evolution.

I will never forget the first time I saw Brad perform. He was playing to several hundred dancing and cheering fans at a club named Cowboys in Arlington, Texas. That night, he insisted I wear one of his cowboy hats (for the first and last time in my life) to get into the spirit of my first country music concert. I remember being impressed with his two tour buses, one of which pulled a small trailer holding all of his show gear. How far he has come! Today Brad has six tour buses, and his little trailer has been replaced with eight semis, each pulling 52-foot trailers to transport the equipment needed to stage his elaborate concerts.

Brad is the creative force behind his concerts, and I've been impressed with how they continue to get better with each successive show. Following his concert at Cowboys, and every concert I've seen since, Brad seeks feedback about his performance, the overall show, and how he and the band can continue to improve. That has impressed me. Here is a person who is good at *how* he does what he does—his fans can attest to that—yet he continues to explore ways to be even better.

As a young artist, Brad knew that to reach his goals he would have to dynamically evolve in all aspects of his craft. And evolve, he has. In 2007 Brad was named both the Academy of Country Music and the Country Music Association's Male Vocalist of the Year. His No. 1 single "Online" won Music Video of the Year. His first CMA nomination was seven years ago, and since that time he has received more nominations than any other artist—38. Brad's sixth CD was released this past year, and the cumulative sales for all of his releases are almost 11 million to date.

Brad headlines in concerts all over North America, and he performed his 1,000th concert this past year to the utter delight of his fans. That crowd of several hundred in Arlington, Texas, has expanded; today he plays in concert halls, auditoriums, and arenas, drawing close to 60,000 fans during a three-night weekend. And fulfilling another of his early goals, Brad's tour is now sponsored by Hershey, a great American brand.

His professional growth has been a delight to observe, but Brad has also grown personally over the past six years. He married Kim, and they have a one-year-old son, Huck. They built a beautiful log cabin home on 85 acres of land they purchased outside of Nashville. He maintains a close relationship with his parents, Doug and Sandy Paisley, which has given me the opportunity to become close friends with them as well.

This past summer, I attended Brad's concert at the Minnesota State Fair in St. Paul. After the tragedy of the bridge collapse, he was the perfect person to bring some joy to that stricken town. Seeing his band is always a treat; and Brent Long, his long-time tour director, always makes me feel welcome. Brad's band has been together for over eight years—a rarity in the music business. Why the loyalty? Because they serve each other extremely well; they serve Brad and Brad serves them. And when service reciprocity exists, the result is loyalty.

Before his performance that evening, I asked Brad what he thought contributed to his continuous evolution and growth over the past six years. He said, it all begins with the music. He understands what the fans need and want, and "if I satisfy those needs with my music, singles hit the top of charts, the CDs sell well, my concerts get bigger, and the fan base grows. But it all begins with the music and how that connects me to the fans."

LESSON TO REMEMBER

In my opinion, Brad's growth and enormous success have
resulted from many of the factors addressed in this book.

- Throughout his career, Brad has stayed true to his
  purpose and values and supports them with his behaviors.
- He understands the needs of all he serves—be they his
  company, his fans, or the country music industry.
- Brad satisfies those needs by getting better at *how* he
  does what he does. His approach has evolved to ensure an
  experience that continuously improves for everyone.
- He seeks continuous feedback from his team and fans, and
  then listens to and acts on their responses.

When I first saw Brad perform in Texas, I knew he had
enormous talent. Six years later, watching him perform in
Minnesota, I was truly moved by the personal and professional
transformation he had worked so hard to achieve by
consistently adhering to the five steps to Service Excellence.

In our final chapters, we will explore the ways in which
companies can undergo the same remarkable transformation.

11

Keep the Culture Growing

Changing the culture requires determination, courage, passion, humility, and recognition; doing the same things in the same ways will not result in profound change.

—Rob Livingston

Transforming your organization into a true service culture is challenging, but equally daunting is the task of ensuring your new culture thrives once embedded. This phase of your Service Excellence transformation requires the constant vigilance of a companywide self-governing body, empowered to guide the evolution. *What* you do may require a hierarchy of responsibility and authority, but when it comes to matters of service (*how*), everyone is equal. So it is essential for your governance body to be composed of people from every level across the company, who function as peers in this capacity.

In a conversation I had with Malcolm Gladwell, the very well-respected author of *The Tipping Point* and *Blink*, we discussed this subject of cultural deep rooting and its inherent challenges. He observed that "cultures can change and can be transformed by small changes in everyone's behavior. Positive behavior is contagious from those around us. Our behaviors are a response to our environment; some people will serve well because that is

who they are. Others will change because the environment encourages it."

He went on to say that, "People within an organization play
critical roles in any culture. It is important to identify and empower the right ones who can consistently provide the service/
social leadership required to get the cultural transformation to
epidemic proportions. Any transformation requires a condition
to spread from one person to the other (a virus) before it reaches,
in this case, a service culture epidemic. Patience is a significant
discipline everyone must adhere to as the culture develops."

In earlier chapters, we described the five steps required to effect a cultural transformation. These steps, proven to be successful, are your blueprint for change. Adherence to the plan cannot
be spotty or optional; mutual goals, cooperative approaches, and
common terminologies will form the foundation of your new
culture. In this chapter, we discuss how to ensure that your new
culture will take root and continue to grow. In the absence of
individual behavioral changes, the culture will not change; but
as behavior modifications flourish, the collective power of these
changes will shape your new culture.

Transformation versus Training

This is *not* a training initiative. A culture change is a *transformational movement.* There will be the need for some mode of education for purposes of informing and clarifying your new approach
to serving internal and external clients. The desire to transform
into a Service Excellence culture must be communicated broadly
and discussed openly, and it must be consistently reinforced from
its inauguration. We have found the most effective approach to
be a series of meetings with all employees to impart this information and address questions. But again, we must stress, this is *not* a
training initiative.

The CROSSMARK transformation, implemented and honed over a number of years, is the experience that enabled us to refine our blueprint. The approach was simple yet comprehensive, and personal yet interconnected. From its inception, and at every stage along the way, CROSSMARK's transformation was supported by its senior leadership. They publicly committed to a five-year start-up plan, from which they never retreated. They asked Jim Borders, their COO at the time, to champion the cultural transformation movement. They retained me and my son Rob to generate awareness and create excitement about this innovative idea. Every action and statement from CROSSMARK's senior management was an endorsement of this cultural transformation.

Creating awareness about a change of this magnitude is essential for your success, but it is a step companies tend to overlook or underestimate. A mass e-mail, voice-mail, or video does not qualify as having fulfilled this important responsibility to your employees. Creating awareness sets the tone and builds the foundation for a successful cultural transformation, and we were fortunate that CROSSMARK understood its importance. Deeming this step most effective when performed by an independent third party, we were selected for our industry experience and credibility in the area of Service Excellence.

This was not a transient step. Estimated to be a three-year venture for CROSSMARK, this phase of the transformation required complex logistics and a great deal of planning. We consulted with CROSSMARK's client services, training, and human resources departments in the development of our awareness-building program, and we initiated pilots with small groups to validate our approach. Upon completion of the pilots, we embarked on our roll-out to their core group of 1,700 full-time associates, geographically dispersed throughout North America.

These 1,700 associates were divided into groups averaging 55 people, with whom we held a series of five full-day cultural awareness meetings over a three-year period. These meetings included every full-time associate at CROSSMARK, regardless of his or her position within the company. Every single person received the same message. And we carefully observed each group to gauge which individuals might require further follow-up.

People being people, this phase required persuasion, proofs of concept, and promises from senior leadership. In an inverse approach to the anticipated skepticism, we thought long and hard about what this transformation was *not*. Who among us has not experienced the cycle of companies' flavor-of-the-month programs that are quickly discarded for the newest sexy business trend? So we clearly understood our obligation to acknowledge the elephant in the room and address what this was *not*.

What Transformation Is *Not*

Upon approval from the CROSSMARK executive management committee, the launch of their cultural transformation became the province of Jim Borders. From the outset, Jim's positioning of the cultural transformation was unmistakable. The company awareness meetings were *not* training sessions, they were *not* designed to teach a new skill, and they did *not* have a specific job-related focus. Rather, these meetings were used to set in motion a cultural transformation that would require the knowledge and participation of everyone. Disassociating this series of meetings from past initiatives was an essential first step. And so (yes, for the third time), it was *not* a training initiative. What else was it *not*?

- A series of seminars
- Exclusionary
- Focused on people's roles
- Short term
- A motivational tool

Transformation Is *Not* a Series of Seminars

CROSSMARK's five cultural awareness meetings facilitated an understanding and familiarity with the concept of Service Excellence; these meetings were never characterized as service seminars. Rather, they provided a forum for becoming conversant in the five steps to achieving Service Excellence, a safe environment for exploring ways to enhance internal and external servicing, and a firm grounding in the ultimate goal of competitive differentiation. Communicating, illustrating, resolving, sharing, validating, and practicing were all ingredients of these meetings.

Predictably, the initial meetings were populated with skeptics, rebels, and people irritated by this interference in their busy schedules of *what*. But after the second phase of the meetings, there was a more prevalent sense that CROSSMARK was serious about a cultural transformation, and alignment progressed. As more people began to understand and experience the benefits of Service Excellence, they climbed on board. Each successive meeting produced greater degrees of acceptance, enthusiasm, and collaboration.

These meetings (referred to as *phases*) were structured to guide people through the five steps to Service Excellence, in the chronological order of our roadmap:

Phase 1.   This introductory meeting launched the cultural transformation, reinforced the support of senior leadership, and outlined the five steps to Service Excellence.

Phase 2.   Six months later, each group reconvened to explore more deeply each step of the roadmap to Service Excellence and to renew their commitment to the cultural transformation.

Phase 3.   The third meeting was devoted entirely to the creation of Service Action Plans. The nature of this work compelled us to meet in smaller groups of 10 to 15 people at a time. In these groups we were able to more thoroughly assess individuals' comprehension of Purpose and Values, dual need forms (hard versus soft), and Service Action Plans. We reviewed the action plans, not only as a reinforcement of learning but also as a positive way to acknowledge and convey the behaviors of those who clearly grasped the concept. The smaller group was a nonthreatening and more effective environment for this in-depth work.

Phase 4.   At the fourth meeting we gathered for the purpose of ensuring a comprehensive understanding and practice of the five steps to Service Excellence. But perhaps more importantly, this meeting initiated the transfer of ownership for the cultural transformation from the governing body to the associates. And lest anyone confuse the transfer of ownership with waning support of senior management, the message of their strong commitment to the cultural transformation was emphasized, as was their expectation of full support and participation from every member of the organization.

Phase 5.   The fifth and final meeting was held with the smaller groups of 10 to 15 people. Again, the focus was on their Service Action Plans. At this meeting the groups hammered out how their service actions needed to evolve through creative behaviors that would continue to raise the bar on service. In this meeting, the new company Service Leaders and local Service Steering Committees were also announced.

To reemphasize, these five meetings were not viewed as seminars or training programs. They were organizational meetings to engage everyone in a service and cultural transformation. This deliberate positioning is the reason the meetings were so successful.

Transformation Is *Not* Exclusionary

Since everyone plays a role in any given culture, it follows that a cultural transformation must involve everyone. Culture is not the domain of the executive ranks. It's astonishing how frequently that little detail is overlooked. The CROSSMARK meetings included every full-time associate, regardless of position or location, and attendance was mandatory. If conflicts arose, people were required to travel to another location. CROSSMARK's objective was to differentiate itself from the competition by creating a service culture in which *every* person in *every* location created a memorable experience for *every* internal and external client, *every* time. Such a lofty goal can be accomplished only when *everyone* owns the transformation and the culture.

Transformation Is *Not* Focused on People's Roles

Service Excellence has *nothing* to do with your position in the company, but it has *everything* to do with your behaviors. Positions are narrowly defined; behaviors are ubiquitous. Discussions about roles and responsibilities, in the context of a cultural transformation, are distractions that will undermine your ability to stay on track and succeed. CROSSMARK was vigilant about staying focused on the five steps to Service Excellence and the correlated behaviors. A fair amount of time was devoted to distinguishing between internal and external clients and to stressing the importance of service action planning for each constituency. This topic was worthy of discussion because all participants understood that *how* they did what they did in serving *internal* associates would heavily influence the success of CROSSMARK's aspirations for their cultural transformation.

Transformation Is *Not* Short Term

The senior leadership of CROSSMARK was overt about their long-term commitment to this cultural transformation. In the words of John Thompson, then president of CROSSMARK Retail, "We are committed to this transformation for an initial period of five years. We believe that within that time frame, the company will have transformed ourselves into the service leader in our industry. In so doing, we will achieve a differentiation that sets us apart from our competitors."

CROSSMARK never doubted that a transformation of this magnitude would require a multiyear commitment to their associates. But the decision wasn't difficult; they were convinced it was an investment that would return significant dividends. If the Service Excellence culture they envisioned came to fruition, CROSSMARK would be a great place to work, client relationships would grow and prosper, the company would outrival competition, and they would build their bridge to loyalty.

Rhetoric comes easily at the outset of a new initiative. Sticking to your commitment is much more difficult, particularly over a span of years. Too many companies suffer from attention deficit, which is the demise of any transformation endeavor. CROSS-MARK is to be commended for an unwavering allegiance to their cultural transformation—for the duration.

Transformation Is *Not* a Motivational Tool

Motivational tools have short shelf lives for most people, and, as we just discussed, making a cultural transformation requires a long-term commitment. We intentionally stayed away from the motivational format for that reason and put some distance between our message and the many excited utterances that have come before. Instead, the transformation was supported by the series of five "awareness meetings," company communiqués, sharing of best practices, and the "on-boarding" of new associates to immerse them, without delay, in the Service Excellence culture.

What Transformation *Is*

We have revealed what transformation is *not*, thereby raising the question, what *is* it?

- A proven and attainable aspiration
- Revolutionary
- Enduring
- All inclusive
- A means to competitive advantage, differentiation, and loyalty
- Senior leadership endorsed but associate owned

We hope these descriptors are familiar to you; they summarize the subject matter of our previous 10 chapters!

Getting Started on Deep Rooting

Our service crisis is so endemic that none among us is spared appallingly bad experiences. If there is a silver lining, it's that selling your people on the benefits of transforming to a service culture will not be difficult. But the actual process of engaging everyone in your transformation will require tremendous determination, commitment, patience, time, and communication.

> At the outset, you must exhibit the unflagging tenacity to make this change permanent.

The CROSSMARK launch meetings were educational and created excitement about the cultural transformation. A benefit of this process was learning that one of the most important messages to impart at this early stage is that a culture of Service Excellence generates competitive advantage. Not only will the business environment improve but also the resulting business gains for the company will create new opportunities for individuals. This message resonated with the majority of people. In an unscientific poll of our launch team, we estimated that close to 80 percent of the CROSSMARK associates were aligned with the precepts of transformation by the end of the launch meetings.

What Happens Next?

You've successfully completed the 100-yard dash; now you're at the starting line of the marathon. With an understanding of the cultural change embedded in the organization, all associates must assume ownership of the transformation and begin to *live* and *own* the culture every single day. What do you look for as confirmation?

- An understanding and observance of the company's Purpose and Values, as evidenced by behaviors
- An understanding of the soft needs of your internal and external clients, as evidenced by Service Action Plans designed to satisfy those needs
- Service Action Plans for everyone with whom people interact 80 percent of the time, and for the constituencies with whom they interact less frequently
- Evidence of continuous improvement, since *getting better at getting better* is the key to individual and company growth

We sincerely believe most people are well intentioned. But as the pile of *what* grows, it's not uncommon to revert to old behaviors. To lessen this natural tendency, senior leadership must systemically support and reward those who live and own the culture. Only when the infrastructure reinforces the culture will you be able to set down deep roots. Many actions are straightforward (for example, if you want to see how people act, look at how they're compensated). Some basic requirements for overtly bolstering your new culture include the following:

Hiring guidelines and criteria that identify service-oriented candidates who will mesh with and support the culture

Performance reviews that evaluate associates' service traits, attitudes, and behaviors in the context of the culture

Bonuses and incentives that are tied to providing Service Excellence

Recognition programs that reward continuous improvement

Salary increases that are tied to providing Service Excellence

How Others Do It

Great service companies share common beliefs about the importance of culture, behaviors, people, and relationships. These beliefs manifest themselves in different ways, but they form the core of each company's operating principles. We caution you against simply copying these tenets because each business is unique and must be approached as such. But there is value in exploring the common threads that run through our benchmark companies and determining their role in establishing your deep roots:

- Everyone is equal in service matters.
- Associates first; customers second.
- Hire for attitude; train for skill.

- Empowerment guides all.
- There are no superstars.
- Rewards and recognition are essential.

Consider the benefits that would accrue to you and your company, were you to embrace those principles.

Everyone Is Equal in Service Matters

Hierarchies are necessary for delineating *what* people do. But in the realm of *how* you do what you do, great service companies believe everyone is equal. This is not inscribed on a wall plaque; it is evidenced, very simply, by their behaviors.

The strongest proof that a company is living this principle can be found in the simple act of empowering their people to creatively deliver great service experiences. Companies who believe everyone is equal in matters of service support common-sense problem resolution, trust people to make sound judgments, and create environments of freedom and amnesty. They institute 360-degree feedback mechanisms, and they seek input from every level of the organization on matters of service, differentiation, and *how* you do what you do.

Associates First; Customers Second

Remember Wegmans, the successful grocery retailer in the Northeast who lives by the motto "Employees first, customers second"? Who could dispute that theirs is a thriving and deep-rooted culture given their 10 consecutive appearances on *Fortune*'s list of Top 100 Companies to Work For?

Are you willing to put your associates first, even if it means sacrificing short-term business goals? The great service companies value an environment in which associates feel important, respected, and well treated. They understand that attitudes and behaviors are contagious and that their treatment of employees will rebound to their clients, who in turn will be made to feel important, respected, and well treated.

Do not mistake this as devaluing your clients' significance in any way. Rather, think of it as a tennis match where the better your partner, the better you play. Great service companies understand that the more they empower and respect their associates, the happier their clients will be.

Perhaps the best way to illustrate this notion of "Associates First" is to look to some of *Fortune*'s Best Companies to Work For in 2007 and see how these practices reflect their cultures, thereby strengthening the deep-rooting process:

Google (No. 1 ranked) offers free gourmet meals daily; allows you to bring your dog to work; provides car wash, free laundry, barber and massage services; pays you $5,000 to buy a hybrid car; has no dress code; has a swimming pool, spa, gyms, and game rooms; and offers free on-site medical care. Engineers can also spend 20 percent of their time on independent projects, which led to the development of Gmail. Is it any wonder they're ranked No. 1?

Genentech (No. 2 ranked) is a biotech leader with uncommonly loyal staffers. "Wild horses could not drag me away," says one employee. Last year 537 employees took six-week paid sabbaticals, available to every associate for each six-year term of service.

The Container Store (No. 4 ranked), a storage products retailer, pays sales employees 50 to 100 percent above industry average. Nearly one-tenth of all employees take advantage of the family-friendly shift, from 9 a.m. to 2 p.m., allowing for school drop-offs and pickups.

Methodist Hospital System (No. 9 ranked) sent all but the top executives a $250 Chevron gift card, in the wake of soaring gas prices. This gesture prompted more than 500 staffers to send thank you e-mails to CEO Ron Girotto.

Qualcomm (No. 14 ranked) encourages their employees to submit new product concepts or any other ideas via the company's online network. Perks include a fitness center, 100 percent health-care coverage, and catered dinner if you work late.

American Century Investments (No. 15 ranked) allows employees to take any course of study, even in a subject unrelated to their job, and reimburses them 75 percent of the tuition. Symphony and theater tickets are reimbursed at 50 percent. And there's heavy investment in training as well: $2,700 per employee.

We came across an interesting statistic regarding a major issue in America today: health-care benefits for employees. Of the Top 100 Best Companies to Work For, 40 percent pay 100 percent of the health-care premiums for their employees. Among the Fortune 500 companies, that number is 14 percent. If you have ever wondered about the extent to which insurance premiums impact an employee's perception of their value, this is telling.

It is really very simple. If you put your associates first, your clients will feel as though they have been put first. This is what great service companies, who sincerely value their associates, do to deep root that part of their culture.

Hire for Attitude; Train for Skill

You have been vigilant about your cultural transformation— holding awareness meetings, discovering your clients' soft needs, composing Service Action Plans, and defining the traits required for successful service people. The last thing you want is to sabotage your progress by hiring people who do not fit well with your culture. This is not to say there's anything wrong with these candidates. It's simply that neither party will be happy, and your cultural transformation will suffer should you engage the services of someone who is not suited to live and own the culture.

This suggests the need for a defined interviewing protocol. The traits you have defined for success must be among the criteria for hiring new people. Conversely, the lack of those traits must be a disqualifier. Interview questions must be designed to discover the presence or absence of prerequisite traits. Interviews should be conducted by multiple people across different disciplines to ensure agreement and consistency in evaluation. Of course, hiring managers should retain authority for the final decision, but members of your company or team should have input into candidates' traits and their cultural alignment.

During one of our awareness meetings, a CROSSMARK associate relayed a story about his neighbor who was interviewing for a store manager position at Whole Foods. This man was astonished that there were very few questions about his previous job. The majority of questions were about behaviors and his relationships with the various communities in his personal life. This is the sign of a company who hires for attitude.

The importance of traits cannot be overemphasized. Ask yourself the following questions to determine the extent to which you're ready to incorporate traits into the selection and evaluation of your associates.

- Are you prepared to identify traits essential to your organization?
- Are you ready to announce those traits to the company?
- Are you primed to make them important in the culture?
- Will traits be used as performance measurements and hiring guidelines?

You may not always succeed in exposing candidates whose traits are inconsistent with your culture, but you can certainly shift the balance in the direction of good hires. In the words of Colleen Barrett, president of Southwest Airlines, *"Do we probably let some good people go that we should hire? Yes. But do we have a good rate of return on those who come through the door? Absolutely."*

Empowerment Guides All

Within logical parameters, service-centric companies empower their associates to make decisions in order to satisfy the needs of those they serve. Great service companies publicly commend associates who proactively address problems even though they may occasionally fail. Their message is, better to step up and act in the best interests of the client than do nothing. Creativity in problem solving is encouraged, limiting the need to ask for permission within reasonable boundaries.

There are actions, some of which are listed below, that you can take to reinforce to your associates that they are empowered to serve their clients:

- Ask associates to write their own service role descriptions, from the perspective of *how* they do their jobs. (*What* they do is already captured in their job descriptions.) Review with team members and senior leadership.
- Encourage managers to actively seek solutions from front-line employees, and publicly acknowledge resulting successes.
- Promote open dialogue across all levels of the company, which also reinforces that everyone is equal in matters of service.
- Grant unfettered access to clients for purposes of improving service.
- Communicate that management owns the business relationship but everyone who touches the client owns the service relationship.
- Issue a written "Empowerment Commitment" statement from senior management, detailing expectations of empowerment and protection from failures (excepting steady patterns of misfortune).

There Are No Superstars

Everyone is equal in matters of service, so it follows that all positions are of equal value, and titles are meaningless. There appears to be an entire subculture devoted to the creation of zany titles; you will laugh at the following list of actual titles we found on various blogs and Web sites. But looking beyond the humor for a moment, you will see how these titles support the principle that attitudes and behaviors (*how*) define you or your company—not skills (*what*).

Chief Evangelist (aka CEO)
Chief People Person (aka human resources director)
Knowledge Officer (aka librarian)
Director of First Impressions (aka receptionist)
Director of Mind and Mood
Chief Imagination Officer
Intangible Asset Appraiser
Creatologist
Director of Intellectual Capital
Chief Morale Officer
Chief Dreamer
Chief Catalyst
Spiritual Capitalist
Ego Enhancement Consultant
Dream Broker
Misconception Eradicator
Spiritual Fulfillment Counselor
Chief Fulfiller of Needs
Impresario of Equalities

An environment that doesn't cotton to superstars has the character and integrity to genuinely respect all positions and levels within the organization. These companies value the success of the culture or team over the success of the individual. A great illustration of this is Nucor Steel:

- All employees are named in the company's annual report.
- Performance-based bonuses are part of everyone's compensation package.
- There are no executive parking spaces.
- Their CEO flies coach class on commercial airlines.
- Their CEO makes 23 times the factory workers' pay (a typical CEO earns 400 times).

Whole Foods is another company who doesn't endorse a cult of "Superstars." They have long capped the salaries of their top executives, currently at 19 times the average full-time pay.

Rewards and Recognition Are Essential

People are motivated by rewards and recognition. Particularly in a service culture, recognition must be creative and meaningful or the result will be the opposite of the desired effect. Slogans and silly trinkets are hollow acknowledgments, and they are best left in the supply cabinet. In recognizing great service, personal attention resonates most with your associates. Remember, personal interactions not only define you; they also satisfy the soft needs of those you are recognizing. Consider the possibilities:

- A personal, handwritten note of appreciation is far more meaningful than an e-mail.
- Public recognition through a Service Excellence communiqué works wonders.
- Praise from and among peers provides great inspiration.
- A team meeting is a great forum for acknowledging and celebrating outstanding service actions.
- Widely sharing recognition from external clients is both appreciated and flattering.

For recognition to be meaningful, listen for cues about what your associates value. Employee satisfaction surveys reveal that people really appreciate time off. Perhaps some off-the-books vacation time would be a marvelous way to reward great service actions. Be open and candid about these kinds of rewards; there should not be any hint that such arrangements were clandestine.

Many great service companies have created a "Service Hall of Fame" spotlighting their high achievers. Display their photos at your company headquarters in visible locations. Hold annual recognition dinners or special appreciation events for those with consistently excellent servicing records. Publicize promotions and job changes at all levels, and use the publicity as a vehicle to communicate tangible proof that individuals committed to Service Excellence achieve upward mobility. Recognize and celebrate each other's successes and milestones. I just received a card from Southwest Airlines celebrating my 10-year anniversary as a frequent flyer member. Unexpected but very much appreciated.

Done well, you cannot overrecognize people and their achievements; done poorly, you can. Be creative, and guard against banal forms of gratitude. Have a filter; don't try to create something where there is nothing. Favoritism has no place in reward and recognition programs. Doing this well requires listening, thinking, creativity, and time, but the upside potential is tremendous.

Storytelling and Ongoing Service Reinforcement

True stories are very powerful and, as the saying goes, often stranger than fiction. In the hands of a good storyteller, successes, challenges, and even failures are potent teaching instruments. Create opportunities to communicate service stories orally. Build the lore of your culture and, in the process, a cultural service language. Seek out internal storytellers to gather or share service knowledge and experiences in some of the following ways:

- Establish service communication vehicles such as videos, newsletters, e-mails, person-to-person meetings (not to be confused with service awareness creation).
- Institutionalize a process encouraging associates, clients, and customers to share service experiences.
- Where applicable, use the wealth of information from your customer service call centers, blogs, and online communities; consumers are amazingly forthright.
- Solicit input and feedback from Service Steering Committees.
- Create a local bulletin board exclusively for recognition.
- Use your organization's Web site to "broadcast" your commitment to Service Excellence.

What Else Can Be Done?

Cultures are simply the shared beliefs, values, and attitudes of a group. Therefore, to embed a new culture in your company, it is essential for every person to understand that everyone else (vertically and horizontally) supports this value system. Some approaches that have proven effective include the following:

- Asking associates to sign a Service Pledge, stating they are "on board"
- Distributing a Service Empowerment Pledge, signed by all senior executives
- Conducting weekly small-group discussions, limited to the topic of service
- Pairing every associate with a "Service Pal" from another area of the company
- Establishing online service communities
- Setting up service "blogs" hosted by internal service leaders

Other Benchmark Companies

We have highlighted many great service companies, focusing on those with whom the majority of people are likely to have interacted, thereby enabling a more personal identification with the behaviors we have examined. But we would be remiss if we did not acknowledge many other great companies with service-based cultures worth experiencing such as the following:

American Girl	Levenger
Bank of America	Netflix
Bristol Farms	Oliver Peoples
Build-A-Bear	Patagonia
Cedars-Sinai Hospital	Publix
Charles Schwab	Smith & Hawken
Chick-fil-A	Talbot's
Corniche Travel	TD Ameritrade
Enterprise	Wachovia Bank
Harley-Davidson	Yum! Brands

We encourage further research on these companies to understand their unique approaches to *how* they do *what* they do.

Obstacles to a Service Excellence Culture Change

As you begin your journey of cultural transformation, you can expect to encounter obstacles along the way. Anticipating these barriers and planning strategies to overcome them will minimize or, better yet, eliminate them from the start. The most common obstacles fall into these areas:

- Timing and pacing
- Internal communications

- Revenue producing versus overhead dissonance
- Senior leadership engagement

Timing and Pacing

Momentum (noun): the motion of a body and its resistance to slowing down. When your cultural transformation gains momentum, it cannot be slowed. The key is *continuous* forward movement, best accomplished through frequent communication and an acceleration of the back-room vehicles we've discussed to build awareness. Deliver on your internal commitments. Stay true to your published schedules. Once your timeline is established, stick to it. Be relentless in your pursuit of Service Excellence, and tell people about your experiences. Give priority to your company's service improvements. These seemingly simple actions will lend credibility to your initiative; the motion of your cultural transformation will increase, and its resistance to slowing down will crumble.

Internal Communications

Be open in all of your communications because doing so will reinforce the tenet that everyone is equal in service matters. There are no secrets. Do not tolerate lapses in any communication, responses to inquiries, or follow-through regarding your transformation. Publish status reports in a timely manner, and with clarity. These actions will satisfy your associates' soft need to be informed.

Exercise great care to ensure that competing priorities and initiatives within your company do not create confusion or conflicts. In the absence of any senior counsel in this area, and the freedom for associates to set their own priorities, consistency and compliance will suffer.

Revenue Producing versus Overhead Dissonance

Internal conflict between the revenue-producing arms of a company and the operational or support functions is universal. This clash has existed since prehistoric man hunted for food and pre-historic woman cooked it. When internal functional groups are allowed to form silos, they isolate and elevate the importance of *what* they do, distracting attention from revenue-producing clients and service-related pursuits.

But when the focus of an entire company becomes serving internal and external clients, these conflicts are put in their proper perspective—petty diversions relative to the goal of Service Excellence. Integrate revenue-producing and support people to address service matters, and you unify factions by establishing a common purpose toward which to work. Integrate service leadership teams with other functions, and deliver the message that the client comes first and everyone serves the client. Recognize that the front lines—those people who own the client relationship—must come first, and solicit feedback on how well they're being served.

Symbolic gestures are effective in transformational movements. Form an Advisory Council, populated by client-facing and functional associates, to meet semiannually with your Executive Committee on service matters. And do not forget to share the dialogue and outcomes of those meetings with everyone.

Senior Leadership Engagement

This is an absolute: the senior leadership of a company must be actively, enthusiastically, and wholly engaged in the cultural transformation, or it will fail. Period. End of conversation.

Go out of your way to be visible, and voice your support. Participate as equals; remember these are service matters. Be active; accept assignments on various service teams around the country. Then listen; don't lead. Set an example by demonstrating *how* you do what you do.

Without visible and meaningful participation by senior leadership, your initiative will lose momentum and fail. Consider the traits and leadership skills of these successful senior executives;

they did not achieve their dreams of Service Excellence by being distant, silent, or reluctant shepherds of their cultures:

> Sergey Brin: Google
> Larry Page: Google
> Bill Gates: Microsoft
> Howard Schultz: Starbucks
> Steven Jobs: Apple
> Bob Wegman: Wegmans Food Markets
> Herb Kelleher: Southwest Airlines
> Bill Marriott: Marriott Hotels
> Jack Welch: General Electric

Begin Simply

As you prepare to embark on your journey to Service Excellence, publish a set of ground rules that will guide the behaviors necessary for a successful cultural transformation. Then, with some degree of fanfare, *Let's get started!*

- Never be dismissive of anyone.
- Never invalidate others' ideas.
- Never be disrespectful to anyone.
- Never refuse to help someone else.
- Always listen and hear.
- Always praise others.
- Always be humble.
- Always be honest and direct.
- Always reply to anyone you serve within 24 hours.

A TERRIFIC LEARNING

My son Rob and I had concluded the last of our CROSSMARK awareness-building sessions, and we were meeting with their senior service leadership team for our final engagement. Their team consisted of Clay Curtis, VP of training and communications; David Peet, VP of field services; and Rodger Fisher, VP of human resources. The purpose of this meeting was to transfer knowledge regarding our work on their Service Steering Committee, outline our thoughts on forming local steering committees, and officially hand over the mantle of ownership for growing and deep rooting the culture within CROSSMARK.

In the middle of our third, and last, afternoon, we took a short break. We reconvened for our summations, and everyone was present except Rodger Fisher. Because tardiness was so out of character for Rodger, we waited to resume the meeting until he arrived. Fifteen minutes later, he rushed in and asked for the floor to announce the reason for his delay.

"I decided to send an e-mail to all of my HR colleagues to demonstrate my desire to serve them. I'd like to read the message to you."

He proceeded: "As you know, my position entitles me to a reserved parking space in our underground garage. Since we are all equal in service matters, I would like to share that privilege with each of you. Effective next week, we will rotate my reserved parking space among everyone in the department, for one week at a time. I will park in an unreserved space, and the rotation schedule will be announced tomorrow."

There was a collective thud, as the chins of Rodger's colleagues hit the conference room table. What a surprising service action that Rodger was performing on behalf of his internal clients!

He is now on his second full rotation of parking space sharing.

LESSON TO REMEMBER

There are three reasons Rodger's service action was exciting: First, he demonstrated creativity and an understanding of the soft needs of those he served: to feel important, special, and recognized. Second, as a senior leader of the company, he did something tangible to validate the tenet that everyone is equal in matters of service. And third, he demonstrated his active engagement in the collective responsibility to keep their culture growing.

12

Who Owns the Culture?

Culture is the life thread and glue that links our past, present, and future.
—J. W. Marriott, Jr.

Quite simply, the culture is owned by everyone, everywhere, at every time. Service Excellence companies know that *how* they act is an outward reflection of their culture, bestowing upon them a unique identity and competitive differentiation. They understand that the guardianship of their culture is everyone's privilege and responsibility. The culture thrives when its members are proud and take ownership for its nourishment.

Transformation is not an end goal; it is the process of change. Upon reaching your destination, you must undertake the momentous task of deep rooting and sustaining your culture. You will become whom you choose to become, through your behaviors. With continued practice, those behaviors will become your cultural way of life. For everyone committed to a cultural transformation, it's encouraging to realize you have significant influence and control over this outcome. You have the power to embrace differentiation through Service Excellence and define your own unique qualities.

So channel your transformational energy into the perpetuation of your newly formed culture. Ensure that everyone everywhere takes responsibility for its growth and endurance. Do not let this achievement slip through your hands because you thought you had arrived. An old Japanese proverb wisely cautions that "when you have completed 95 percent of your journey, you are only halfway there."

Reflect, once again, on your personal experiences with companies like The Container Store, Marriott, Nordstrom, and Southwest Airlines. Isn't it clear that every employee of these great service organizations owns and lives the culture? And it bears repeating: these same companies have differentiated themselves through Service Excellence, they have secured a competitive advantage and market leadership position in their fields, and all have enjoyed marvelous financial returns. What happens when your associates don't take ownership of the culture? You risk, in the words of Mitchell Habib, the EVP of Global Business Services for The Nielsen Company, "becoming known for the *least best* thing you do." Hardly a noble aspiration.

The behaviors of successful Service Excellence companies are guided by an ideology.

• Nordstrom's Ideology •

Our commitment is 100 percent to customer service. We are not committed to financial markets. We are not committed to real estate markets. We are not committed to a certain amount of profit. We are only committed to customer service. If we make a profit, that's great. But customer service is first. If I'm a salesperson on the floor and I know that the people who own this place are committed to customer service, then I know I won't be criticized for taking care of a customer. I will only be criticized if I don't take care of the customer.

—John Nordstrom

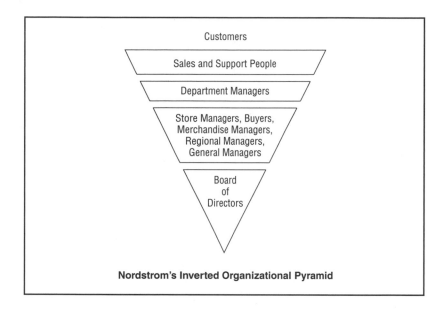

Nordstrom's Inverted Organizational Pyramid

Nordstrom's ideology is represented by their "upside down" pyramid. Take note of who is on top (Robert Spector and Patrick D. McCarthy, *The Nordstrom Way*, p. 98).

• Southwest Airlines' Ideology •

If our employees don't feel good about their work environment and don't feel they have the tools to do their job, what kind of exchange are they going to have with our passengers?

—Colleen Barrett, President, Southwest Airlines

This is reminiscent of our discussion regarding "Associates first, customers second." Since their founding over 40 years ago, this was Herb Kelleher's ideology for Southwest, to which he and Colleen Barrett remain committed today. If you have ever flown Southwest

Airlines, you can't help but notice that every one of their associates appears uncommonly happy, and even when you try to resist, it's contagious.

• Marriott's Ideology •

> The strength of Marriott's teamwork ethic simply means that we've successfully created an environment where the rewards for working together outweigh those of working for one's own interest. Among other things, we must continue to build and maintain a corporate culture that values success but remains capable of critical self-analysis.
>
> —J. W. Marriott

Their culture, under the untiring leadership of Bill Marriott, continues to sustain and grow itself through the ownership of their associates worldwide. This ownership spreads from brand to brand, most recently in collaboration with Ian Schrager as they infuse the Marriott culture into the "boutique" hotel market.

• The Container Store's Ideology •

> At The Container Store, we continue to lead the storage and organization niche that we created by offering our customers solutions, not just products. We do this by selling the hard stuff—by truly involving ourselves, heart and soul, in our customers' needs, which results in amazing interactions between each of our customers and The Container Store's salespeople.
>
> —Kip Tindell, President, The Container Store

This relative newcomer to the distinguished group of Service Excellence companies knew, from the start, that their differentiation was not going to be found in their product line. Service Excellence became their differentiator, and they have become known for their dedication to hiring, training, and motivating great people.

This is an organization that lives by the principle "Hire for attitude, train for skill." They believe in this formula:

1 average person = 3 lousy people

1 good person = 3 average people

1 great person = 3 good people

Their compensation is significantly above the industry average, for both full- and part-time associates. In an industry that averages 7 hours per year of employee training, The Container Store associates receive 185 hours of training in their first year. They refer to their part-time employees as "prime-timers," acknowledging that they work during the busiest hours of the day and deserve respect. And the result is significantly lower employee turnover. The retail industry averages 74 percent, whereas The Container Store has an enviable 28 percent turnover rate.

So Who Owns Your Culture?

The answer is that everyone, everywhere owns your culture, but it does not occur simply by willing it to be so. At the very beginning of your cultural transformation, you must set the expectation that everyone will have the responsibility—and yes, the privilege—of owning the culture. Never shy away from or neglect to deliver this message. But we also advise you to form a core group of *Service Leaders* from your company who have accountability for guiding the culture.

In their book *Nuts! Southwest Airlines' Crazy Recipe for Business and Personal Success*, Kevin Freiberg and Jackie Freiberg describe the Southwest Airline's Culture Committee. This is viewed as Southwest's most important committee, and it is composed of remarkable associates who are great storytellers and Southwest zealots. The committee members, known as "Big Hearts," are selected for their creativity, expertise, energy, enthusiasm, and "Southwest Spirit." They do not seek public recognition. Their role is to ensure the culture is perpetuated and consistent in all parts of the company, from headquarters to local markets. Herb Kelleher describes some of the unique qualities they look for in a Southwest employee: "We like mavericks—people who have a sense of humor. We've always done it differently."

So how do you take this first step toward owning the new culture? How do you make sure others are fully engaged? When do you begin? You begin the very moment you feel the culture is formed, and you empower a network of people who live and own the culture to ensure observance by everyone.

Who Are Service Leaders?

The most effective system is one in which there are *hub* (headquarters-based) and *spoke* (local) *Service Leaders*:

- At the *hub* is a committee composed of no more than five Service Leaders, selected from the ranks of senior management for their passion and renowned reputations as "service zealots." Their role is to ensure that all back-room support programs required to guide the culture have been established and are operational. At the risk of sounding moderately hierarchical, their senior roles also enable them to influence other functional areas whose support is required to sustain the culture: human resources, communications, customer service, training, and administration. This headquarters-based team reports to one member of the company's board of directors, ensuring visibility and alliance at the highest level.

- The *spokes* are individual Service Leaders in each division, office, or local market, depending on the structure of your company. Collectively, they form the companywide Service Steering Committee, but they also receive support from a local Service Steering Committee of their peers. Their roles are to assume local leadership and ownership of the culture and to be the link that ensures universal understanding, communications protocols, and consistent service practices across the company. They are the instrument for continuous feedback, which is a necessity for sustaining ownership of the culture. The spokes are each connected to one member of the hub, facilitating visibility and alliance for all local offices.

What Are Service Steering Committees?

Service Steering Committees are entrusted with the guardianship of the culture and the advancement of cultural ownership; they operate at both a companywide and local level.

From a practical standpoint, these committees ensure the accurate understanding and application of the five steps to Service Excellence. This includes monitoring the quality of service behaviors, engaging everyone in continuous improvement efforts, reviewing and providing coaching on Service Action Plans, and publicizing exemplary service actions and results.

From a managerial standpoint, these committees are responsible for conflict resolution, leading local service meetings, assisting in candidate interviews to determine fit with the culture, and administering and ensuring the consistency of local reward and recognition programs. These committees also assist in the creation of a company service language, which we will discuss later in this chapter.

Selecting the Service Steering Committee Members

This governance body is composed of representatives from each of the constituencies served by the committee; consequently, every job function will have a seat on some or all of your Service Steering Committees. Committees should have no fewer than 3 and no more than 8 people, depending on the group they represent. A good rule of thumb is 1 committee member for every 15 to 20 associates.

Select your representatives carefully; these are the people entrusted with the guardianship of your culture:

- Use service traits to choose enthusiastic volunteers who are fully engaged and supportive of the initiative.
- Select members who are committed to a Service Excellence culture; they are your role models.
- Seek people who are respected in the organization and considered to be influencers.

Other details:

- Committee members should serve a minimum of one year, but they can be rotated every two to three years.
- Local Service Leaders will remain in place since they are the local point of responsibility and accountability.

Guiding the Service Steering Committee Members

Having followed our advice regarding the selection of your Service Steering Committee members, you now have the benefit of working with a tremendously dedicated, enthusiastic, service-oriented group of highly respected individuals. Now it is your responsibility to position them for success by clearly defining and communicating the responsibilities of this new role. The following are important tasks of the Service Steering Committees although, given the wide range of individual situations, some are likely to be more important than others. That prioritization must be exercised by the committees.

1. Develop a service recognition approach.
2. Institutionalize Service Action creativity brainstorming.
3. Resolve internal conflicts.
4. Resolve external conflicts.
5. Develop your service language.
6. Conduct local service meetings.
7. Stamp out bureaucracy.
8. Define cultural leadership responsibilities and expectations.
9. Teach, participate in, and support your "hire-for-attitude" process.
10. Administer Service Excellence activities on a local level.
11. Facilitate dialogue on the development of all support programs.

The first seven points are worthy of additional commentary.

Develop a Service Recognition Approach
Service recognition must be one of your top priorities. The devil is in the details of recognition programs, so be comprehensive, meticulous, and clear about your parameters for rewarding Service Excellence. Consult the experts, if need be. Launch your program with great fanfare. Create excitement about the reward incentives, and be sure to make them significant. Share your plans for publicizing *service heroes*. Solicit ongoing feedback regarding all aspects of the program, and address common themes immediately.

Institutionalize Service Action Creativity Brainstorming
We have emphasized the importance of creativity in achieving true Service Excellence, and we have yet to encounter anyone who takes issue with our point of view. But we've encountered a lot of people reluctant to engage in the creative process. "I'm not creative," "I don't have a creative bone in my body," and "I leave creativity to someone else" are all common reactions. From the

very outset, your Service Leaders must eliminate the apprehension of participating in brainstorming sessions; these sessions will yield a mother lode of creative ideas.

Some quick research uncovered a range of 3 to 10 rules for productive brainstorming sessions. The most common include active participation from every person; no compliments, criticisms, or comments allowed; build on others' ideas; quantity is better than quality; encourage wild ideas; and record everything. There is a wealth of information that is readily available on this subject, and it should be recommended reading prior to hosting your first brainstorming session.

One final thought for the naysayers: The TQM era produced an enormous number of quality improvements to our work processes. Brainstorming was at the very center of that practice; it works. Direct the same energy you expended for uncovering process improvements to generating creative service actions and you will be well along the path to Service Excellence.

Resolve Internal Conflicts

When internal conflicts arise over service-related matters, the Service Steering Committees serve as adjudication bodies; this governance is regarded as one of their central roles. They work to resolve conflict by providing service-based feedback and coaching. The local Service Leaders have accepted accountability for owning and growing the culture, so it is considered their responsibility to bring matters of noncompliance to the attention of the Service Steering Committees. The benefit of centralizing this process is that patterns of noncompliance can be identified, and the root cause can be solved at a macro level.

Resolve External Conflicts

When external conflicts arise over service-related matters, a different solution may be required. The test of great service cultures resides in how they deal with external conflict as well as internal conflict.

Remember what happened to Starbucks in early 2008? Their culture came under fire for "having slipped and gotten away from their basics." The Starbucks culture is sustained through attention, care, and concern for their "baristas," who own the culture and are its reflection with every transaction.

It is likely you've interacted more frequently with Starbucks than with our other benchmark companies. To us, the baristas *are* the Starbucks culture. By owning and living that culture, the baristas are one of the reasons why we visit as often as we do.

Now, *how* they do what they do, as well as *what* they do, was being challenged. How did Starbucks react? They never denied the conflict; they took ownership of it and were proactive in putting in place a solution. Howard Schultz returned as CEO.

In an unprecedented move Schultz closed 7,100 of their stores nationwide for three hours on February 26, 2008, in order to "retrain" 135,000 in-store employees. The day before the closings Schultz said this in a companywide communiqué on the company's Web site: "Tomorrow evening, we will come together in an unprecedented event in our company's storied history. We will close all of our U.S. company-operated stores to teach, educate, and share our love of coffee and the art of espresso. And in doing so, we will begin to elevate the Starbucks Experience for our customers."

Solid customer centered cultures survive conflict by addressing it head on. If the cultures are strong and "owned by everyone," they will survive this difficult time and refocus on how they do what they do.

Time will tell, but I believe Starbucks will be fine! They live their values and are guided by their beliefs.

You can't build loyalty on the outside until you build it on the inside.

—Howard Schultz

Develop Your Service Language

Great service cultures have many common characteristics, but one of the most enjoyable to study is their use of sometimes witty, always unique service languages. These develop as the culture grows, and they may even be adopted by customers as the "language of the land" when interacting with these companies.

This is a great opportunity to deliberately define your culture. Your corporate language must reflect your commitment to Service Excellence. The Service Steering Committees should develop your unique lexicon and then use it broadly and consistently in all forms of communication. In Chapter 11, we had a bit of a chuckle over some unusual job titles, but many of these cleverly illustrated the aspects of a culture, including service goals, humility, and a sense of humor.

In the context of our five steps to Service Excellence, you now understand the specific meaning of *soft needs* and *traits*. These are just a couple examples of a service language; it is up to you to define your culture and support its tenets through the use of your own unique service lexicon. To ignite your thinking, the following are some examples of the service language used by our benchmark companies:

Disney's lexicon. Customers are "guests," and employees—from street sweepers to the CEO—are "cast members." Public areas are "on stage," and restricted areas are "off stage." Every cast member must be "in character" while on stage. Language use is mandatory.

Ritz-Carlton's lexicon. When approached by a guest with a question or request, the compulsory response is "It would be my pleasure."

Starbucks' lexicon. "Baristas" and "partners" describe positions and employees. "Tall," "grande," and "venti" have taken the place of "small," "medium," and "large." "The Green Book" and "The

Green Apron" are their employee manuals. "Star Skills" is how they treat one another. The service interaction always begins with, "What can I get started for you?" In this example, the lexicon creates differentiation.

Southwest Airline's lexicon. They send "Luv notes," and use "Luv lines" in their communications. They refer to themselves as "Big Hearts." Their clothing is called "Fun Wear." Through their sense of humor, they believe "Ha Ha leads to A-ha."

Conduct Local Service Meetings

Constant reinforcement of the culture is absolutely critical for creating the sense of ownership and commitment to growth that will ultimately sustain Service Excellence. Particularly in the early stages, this simply does not occur through osmosis. You must be deliberate and focused in your efforts to grow and nourish your new culture. We have found the most effective means to be regularly scheduled meetings, during which the Service Leaders review and reinforce all aspects of the cultural transformation. This is an opportunity to ensure understanding, verify compliance, and reaffirm everyone's commitment to Service Excellence.

These meetings can be held daily, weekly, or at a minimum, monthly. They must focus exclusively on the service culture and on *how* you do what you do. Guard against natural tendencies to discuss *what* you do and its inherent tribulations; it is a slippery slope. Instead, use these meetings as forums for sharing service success stores, failures in service processes, brainstorming creative service approaches, obtaining feedback, and assessing your overall state of service. Other fruitful discussion areas may include these:

- Internal and external conflict resolution
- Best-practice sharing
- Service Action Plan development, reviews, or revisions

- Recognition of your great service people
- Cross-functional sharing and learning
- Review of your Purpose, Values, and traits

Stamp Out Bureaucracy

Bureaucracy is the death of all sound work.

—Albert Einstein

Best Buy is one of America's largest home entertainment, music, and electronics retailers. Several years ago, much to their dismay, they became well known for their rigidity and dispassionate attitudes in their interactions with customers. In response, Best Buy instituted a program they call ROWE ("Results Only Work Environment"). It was designed to eliminate the bureaucracy that was translating into inflexible rules and creating customer and employee dissatisfaction. The result: turnover has fallen dramatically and productivity has increased 35 percent since 2005 (Michelle Conlin, "Smashing the Clock," *BusinessWeek*, December 1, 2006).

Southwest Airlines addresses bureaucracy via the structure of their chain of command. They allow no more than four layers of management between a front-line supervisor and the president of the company. Empire builders are not welcome. They believe bureaucracy exhausts the entrepreneurial spirit, slows down the organization, and teaches associates to transfer responsibility.

If a policy or practice appears to violate the intent of the company's mission or is inconsistent with its values, people are expected to speak up (Kevin Freiberg and Jackie Freiberg, *Nuts*, p. 130).

With ownership comes responsibility. But in a developing culture, it is that very ownership—by everyone, everywhere, at every time—that will ultimately sustain the new culture you have worked so diligently to create.

A LUXURIOUS LEARNING

Four Seasons is the embodiment of Service Excellence. Dedicated to perfecting the travel experience with their elegant surroundings, round-the-clock personal service, and attentive staff, they represent the highest standards in hospitality. Their associates are inextricably bound and inspired by their singular focus on living the Four Seasons culture. For those travelers who know and appreciate the very best, Four Seasons offers a true home-away-from-home experience.

Founded in 1960, today Four Seasons has 74 hotels in 31 countries, and in 2007 the company had more than 25 new properties under development. They have charted and adhered to a purposeful expansion strategy, targeting major cities and desirable resort destinations around the world. Admirably, they have melded growth with innovation, constantly defining new ways to make business travel easier and leisure travel more memorable.

Opened in 1987, the Four Seasons Hotel Los Angeles is located in a quiet palm-lined residential neighborhood of Beverly Hills, just minutes from the elegant shopping district on Rodeo Drive. The hotel exudes luxury, but it does so with a relaxed California ambience. Known for their impeccable service, the staff exhibits a dedication to the Four Seasons culture that you see in everyone, everywhere, and at every time.

I first stayed there in the early stages of considering a sales incentive trip in which the winners would attend the Rose Bowl in 1989. That planning trip was the first time I met some Four Seasons associates: Mehdi Eftekari, Carol Watkins, Ephrem (who goes by one name), Dale Brunner, and Dana Bronson, most of whom were on site when the hotel first opened at that location.

I recall being impressed with every person's awareness of and respect for their culture; it governed the hotel. More remarkable was the way in which they lived the Four Seasons company culture but refined and adapted that culture to accommodate their high-profile and demanding guests who sought a casual environment. I have had the pleasure of returning to this hotel many times in the past decade, and that devotion to their culture is even truer today.

Recently, I had the opportunity to discuss the notion of "owning a culture" with some of the hotel's long-term associates. In particular, I was impressed with the way in which their culture appeared to grow stronger as the hotel matured, and I asked for their perspective on how this had evolved. Sarah Cairns, the Four Seasons' director of public relations, observed that "120 of our 550 associates have been here since we opened. That's remarkable, isn't it?"

Building on that thought, Carol Watkins, the director of entertainment sales, explained, "With that many people who have been here from the start, our culture has strengthened with the passage of time. We are successful because we know how to communicate with one another. Each of us has a great sense of ownership in the culture, and we have learned to be certain that an individual's part in the service experience is perfect and supportive of one another."

Emphasizing the importance of communication, Carol added that, "Everyone trusts everyone else to deliver their part of the service experience. All that is required is clear, direct communications." To illustrate this point, Carol shared a recent exchange she'd had with Avi, the food and beverage manager, which is now coined "The Wasabi Pea Intervention":

> "I called Avi, and asked if we could get some of the wasabi peas we used to have as bar snacks. I shared that my client, Nicolette, loved them and would be coming to the hotel in a few days.
>
> "Avi explained that the hotel had stopped carrying the peas since the distributor required a 25-case minimum purchase, far in excess of their demand. So he said it would be much easier for him to run to Bristol Farms (a local grocer) and buy them there.
>
> "I replied that Nicolette was dreaming about these wasabi peas so having someone buy them at Bristol Farms was a great idea, and I thanked him.
>
> "Avi's reply? Done!"

Like a complex machine, everyone, everywhere, at every time has a specific individual contribution to the total service experience. Clear communications and trust ensure a well-oiled machine. These owners and champions of the culture at Four Seasons LA understand the connectivity that each has to the whole. Ephrem and Dale Brunner have both been with the hotel since its opening.

Ephrem, the most senior bellman, takes his role very seriously. "I am responsible for first impressions," he explains. "In most instances, I am the first person to greet our guests upon arrival and the last person to bid our guests good-bye upon departure.

"I need to be certain all of our guests feel welcome, at home, and comfortable in their rooms. I am also the first problem solver if the room, the view, or the location does not meet a guest's expectations. As I get them settled, or assist in their departure, I listen carefully for information that should be communicated to others on our staff, anything that will be helpful for this or future stays."

Dale Brunner is a server in the Gardens, the Four Seasons' fine dining restaurant. Dale is the most superb professional server I have encountered in all my years of traveling and dining out. His restaurant is frequented by hotel guests but also by a number of "regulars" who live and work locally. Dale truly enjoys his work, and he takes seriously the role he plays in their guests' overall experience. His unwavering commitment to Service Excellence has earned Dale recognition as Employee of the Month many times over, and he is the only associate at this location to have twice been awarded the honor of Employee of the Year.

Dale began our conversation about how he does what he does by saying, "I consider it a privilege to serve guests in this magnificent environment. This culture is truly wonderful, and I have learned a tremendous amount just from working with such fine people these past 20 years. I have been taught so much by the Four Seasons, its culture, and our guests that, with the passage of time, I truly believe I have come to live my entire life as a better person. The Four Seasons' way of life—how we treat one another and our guests—has become my way of life, all the time."

Dale talked about understanding the needs of his guests this way: "Everyone is different, so I always try to understand, even anticipate, what will make their experience most memorable. Sure, they all need a great meal; that's what our restaurant provides. But each guest has other needs that must be considered. That is why 'how' I serve them matters greatly to them and to me. I seek perfection with every service encounter."

Finally, Dale expanded on something he calls "glitch recovery" and what Carol Watkins referred to as "saving the day." Every associate has been trained to be sensitive to problems, instructed to communicate them broadly, empowered to do whatever it takes to immediately resolve a problem in favor of the guest, and recover the positive experience.

Confirming that "glitch recovery" or "saving the day" is indeed pervasive at Four Seasons, Dana Bronson discussed this concept with me at length. Dana is the director of entertainment, who has also been with the hotel since its opening in 1987. He is an outside contractor who, for the past 20 years, has arranged music programs for guests and local residents every Thursday, Friday, and Saturday.

"From the earliest days, our philosophy has been that people want to relax and enjoy live entertainment—not something 'piped in.' That supports our culture, doesn't it? It is all about personal interactions."

Dana went on to talk about the importance of ownership and how, when a situation occurs that may develop into a bad experience for a guest, every-one is trained to take ownership of the situation and see it through to a sat-isfactory conclusion; they are not to hand it off to someone else. He cited three interesting illustrations of what he describes as "ownership recovery":

"So often a band is selected to perform at a wedding reception but, with the ceremony, the music itself has been overlooked. I get a last-minute call from the hotel, and off I go with music book in hand, and two of my colleagues who are on call, to form an instant classical ensemble."

Dana's second illustration involved another wedding when he overheard a request the couple was making for a silk pillow for the ceremony. "I stepped in, let them know I had just received three white silk pillows as a gift, and I went home to get one for their ceremony—thus, saving their day!"

One of Dana's most memorable experiences began at midnight on a Sunday, the quietest night in the hotel business. He received a phone call from the hotel's restaurant manager requesting that Dana come immediately to the hotel, saying, "Frank Sinatra is coming here from a televised taping of his 80th birthday celebration, and he wants to cap off the night with some music and close friends."

Dana was exhausted; he had been in a recording studio all day and playing at a private party all evening. "I thought he was kidding and I went back to sleep. But 15 minutes later the hotel manager called again saying that Mr. Sinatra was due to arrive and where was I?

"I quickly put on a suit and headed to the hotel. When I arrived, there was Frank Sinatra by the piano with Tony Bennett, Steve Lawrence, Eydie Gorme, Gregory Peck, and a few others, all waiting to hear me play some old songs."

"Where the hell have you been?" asked Mr. Sinatra.

Dana played piano until 3:30 in the morning, while Frank Sinatra recounted stories about each of the songs he played. Not only was the night saved, but it was magical for a very special guest.

Dana summarized our conversation, sharing thoughts that were sounding more and more familiar as I gathered people's stories. "I have played in many venues and for many different types of crowds. Nothing compares to the experience of this hotel. Everyone works as a team to be certain the guest experience is always the best it can be. We are successful because all of us on the team work together at owning the guest experience."

Mehdi Eftekari, the Four Seasons LA general manager, eloquently shared his personal commitment to living their culture, and responsibility for its nurturing.

"The overall structure of the culture is set by the Four Seasons. The general manager and staff at a particular location then go about understanding the needs of that location's guests so they can adapt and refine the culture further, in order to blend in with the local environment.

"When I first joined the Four Seasons just after Los Angeles opened, I was overwhelmed by the power of the culture that was taking form from the very outset. The associates, who were here seven months before me, made my welcome very comfortable and pleasant."

Mehdi believes that the tone for the culture begins with him. He is the role model for all associates and guests. He knows all of the associates and as much about their families as possible. He makes it his ongoing responsibility to get to know as many of the guests as he can, especially those who remain loyal and continue to return. This hotel has a remarkable loyalty return rate of 60 percent, exceptionally high in the hospitality industry.

One of Mehdi's considerable obligations to the culture is ensuring that new associates who join the company will be a good fit. He personally interviews every new hire, and he is the final of five interviewers who meet with each applicant. He does not focus on the new hire's role at the hotel; he is concerned only with *how* they will do what they will do.

"When I meet a potential new hire, I try to understand the passion they will have for serving our guests. I judge how well they communicate, how well they will represent the Four Seasons, and, most importantly, how well they will fit within our culture."

Mehdi takes his responsibility as "caretaker of the culture" very seriously. He is wholly appreciative of the role everyone, everywhere plays in his hotel. He recognizes that every time an associate interacts with a guest, there is the potential for a shortfall in Service Excellence. But if they bring the right people into the culture, those who demonstrate the traits to "recover," the culture will endure just as it has for the past 20 years at this magnificent location.

LESSON TO REMEMBER

Hotels in the hospitality industry all provide accommodations, banquet space, meeting rooms, and restaurants; *what* they do is very similar. But *how* they do what they do can be a differentiator and the bridge to loyalty. The Four Seasons Los Angeles at Beverly Hills has achieved excellence in both *what* they do and *how* they do it. Try it the next time you are in Los Angeles.

13

So Once Again, Why Change?

The title of this chapter "So Once Again, Why Change?" is for those of our readers who may not yet be convinced of the benefits of a service-based culture. We believe the results obtained by the four professional services companies described in this chapter will put that question to rest. These companies have differentiated themselves through Service Excellence, and doing so has enabled them to build a large base of loyal clients and excel in highly competitive industries. Have they embraced every single idea we've put forth? Not everything. But do they all adhere to the core beliefs we've presented as crucial to a service transformation and your ultimate success? The answer is a definitive yes!

To provide a more in-depth examination of *how* they do what they do, we researched and interviewed the four companies described in this chapter because they are renowned for providing Service Excellence to their clients. These companies all play in the professional services sector, serving other business entities in relatively crowded competitive fields. Consequently, differentiation is critical to their success, and each has achieved this goal through an omnipresent culture of Service Excellence.

These profiles will further validate our view that Service Excellence is a means to competitive differentiation and, ultimately, the bridge to loyalty. In reading each of these profiles, you will recognize the specific service behaviors and actions described earlier in this book. You will appreciate the roles that Purpose and Values play in each company's culture. You will identify with the importance of a culture owned and lived by all and the ways in which the collective behaviors of their associates have defined each company.

Our first profile is of Efficient Collaborative Retail Marketing (ECRM), which provides an innovative business process for streamlining the sales and marketing supply chain in the consumer packaged goods industry. Henry & Horne is the subject of our second profile; they are the largest privately held accounting firm in Arizona, acknowledged as one of the best places to work in the state. Our third profile is of TBWA\Worldwide. This leader in the advertising industry is a true innovator in the art of combining world-class client service with top-level creative development and execution. The final profile is of Accenture, a company that has undergone a dramatic evolution from their modest origins at Arthur Andersen to the global powerhouse of today.

All of these profiles validate that *how* you do what you do will define who you will become.

• The ECRM Story •

What They Do

Efficient Collaborative Retail Marketing (ECRM) is a business process that streamlines the sales and marketing supply chain for manufacturers and retailers operating within the consumer packaged goods industry. From its inception, ECRM conceived of a more efficient and effective forum for buyers and sellers to communicate within the structure of existing industry conventions and meetings. By curtailing the "meet-and-greet" aspects of these gatherings and turning the focus on the transactional benefits for buyers and sellers, ECRM believed they could create an enhanced meeting experience for all constituents.

ECRM's solution was to create an environment of properly structured, rigidly focused, and highly effective private meetings between buyers and sellers, in which discussion would be limited to a single category or season of the merchandising year. As simple as this may sound, the approach was indeed innovative. These sessions became known as Efficient Promotion Planning Sessions (EPPS). ECRM's sophistication grew with the introduction of technology that enabled participants to improve their efficiency and speed to market, enhanced by significant cost and time savings from the elimination of numerous geographically dispersed sales calls. But from the outset, ECRM recognized that innovation was not the key to long-term loyalty and client retention; achieving that goal was dependent on *how* they did what they did . . . *the experience.*

In its formative years, ECRM experimented with various formats and processes. From its inaugural meeting to this day, ECRM's founder and CEO Charlie Bowlus has been zealous about keeping the "meeting experience" top of mind. ECRM's business process has evolved in response to the ever-growing demand for EPPS meetings, but the process improvements are designed to further enhance the meeting experience. Charlie attributes the expanding ranks of loyal clients attending yearly EPPS meetings to "*how* they do what they do."

They Are Cheaper, Faster, and BETTER!

Earlier in the book, we discussed how technology can fail Service Excellence when it accomplishes "cheaper and faster" at the expense of "bettering" the relationship. ECRM is a benchmark service company because they have successfully used transformational technology to make the buyer-seller relationship cheaper, faster, *and better.*

Let me illustrate this point by sharing some details about how EPPS meetings are conducted. The consumer packaged goods industry defines "seasonal categories" as groups of products with a preponderance of sales during a concise period of time, typically framed by an event. Examples include holiday candy (Valentine's Day, Easter, Halloween, and Christmas); sun care products; health aids (cough and cold remedies, allergy medications); fragrances; and school supplies. ECRM defines and standardizes category criteria for the more than 50 meetings they hold each year, and they relay the information to all participants. Each EPPS meeting is an opportunity for retailers to evaluate a large segment of products within a single category, and their corresponding seasonal promotional plans, at one time, in one location. Over the course of three days, buyers and sellers representing most of the major trading partners conduct 50 to 60 individual meetings to discuss merchandising plans and strategies for the upcoming season.

The advantages to both parties are abundant. Retailers are able to focus on specific categories or seasons nine months prior to their peak selling cycle. It facilitates a retailer's ability to take a comprehensive view of a category or season and to make more efficient planning and product placement decisions based on information pertaining to new items and merchandising plans.

So let's return to the issue of technology. ECRM has developed a state-of-the-art platform for use by all participants in the planning and execution of their EPPS meetings. From their preattendance preparation materials, to their on-site premeeting briefings, and to the actual meetings, all accompanied by an extensive feedback process to ensure continuous improvement, the EPPS event Web site guides you through every step of the process. This is what they do cheaper, faster, and better.

ECRM's Purpose

ECRM is a passionately committed team, dedicated to providing a truly exceptional client experience in a fun and friendly atmosphere. Innovation, integrity, and efficiency form the axis on which the experience revolves.

ECRM's Values

Values are the guidelines that direct your behavior, and these are ECRM's:

- They embrace integrity, honesty, and sincerity in their relationships with their clients and teammates.
- They are committed to radical, revolutionary change every day.
- They are driven to expect excellence from one another.
- They embrace cultural diversity and individuality.
- They aggressively seek out opportunities to give back to their communities.
- They understand that profitability is essential to their future growth.
- They are dedicated to actively developing each other and celebrating each other's successes.
- Passion ensures their clients' success.

To achieve true Service Excellence, we know absolutely that the senior leadership of a company must be visible champions of their service culture. ECRM is led by a team of experienced executives who understand the needs of those they serve and have designed a service model that far surpasses the alternatives. Their model creates a client experience that differentiates ECRM from the many consumer packaged goods organizations who host conventions, meetings, and forums. ECRM's business process saves the industry time and money and brings efficiency to the buyer-seller relationship, resulting in a better outcome for all parties.

Charlie Bowlus, their CEO, John Dowers, their president, Jim Rice, their chief information officer, and Mitch Bowlus, their chief financial officer, all share a common vision for the company and their clients. Their leadership style is straightforward, they are proactive in finding solutions, and all are eager to do "whatever it takes" to improve the client experience. Business process improvement is always top of mind, but this executive leadership team is committed to process improvement as a means for improving the client experience, not simply for its own sake.

ECRM's Culture

Creativity, suggestions, and new ideas are encouraged by management. They challenge employees to never be content or satisfied with the status quo but rather to continually look for new ways to improve the client experience. They learn from and cherish their past, but ECRM is a visionary company, always looking to the future to enrich their capabilities and enhance the client experience. While emphasizing the importance of a strong work ethic, ECRM also promotes a fun, fast-paced work environment with the opportunity to learn new skills and advance to any level of the company. This is what defines their culture.

In addition to a unique and exciting business concept, ECRM employs an exceptional group of people who CEO Charlie Bowlus credits for the company's success. "Team" and "family" are commonly used in reference to their associates. The ECRM family has a strong culture built on their Purpose and Values; they are friendly, dedicated, self-motivated, and passionate individuals who constantly strive for excellence in their work. Team members are expected to maintain a can-do attitude and hold their clients second to none. The team environment manifests itself in constant collaboration among employees and in coworkers' going out of their way for one another. Their Cleveland headquarters office is invigorated by a constant flow of energy; smiles abound, and responses such as "no problem!" and "be sure to let me know if you need anything else" are commonplace (their language of service).

ECRM believes that good communication is a vital factor in the smooth and efficient operation of their business. Associates are in constant communication with clients through phone calls, e-mails, and personal discussions at EPPS events. The belief that "the client is always right" is pervasive. The priority of ECRM team members is their clients—ensuring that they have what they need, their problems are solved, and they are having a terrific experience. Employees realize the importance of getting their work done in a timely, accurate manner, as it can affect the team's performance.

At EPPS events, all team members attend the evening dinner functions and interact with clients. These events satisfy the needs for both parties to meet and greet one another. If a client issue arises that a team member is unable to solve, they are encouraged to deliberate with another teammate to find a solution. ECRM believes there is a solution to every problem, and their people are empowered to bring that belief to life.

The energy, passion, and commitment that emanates from the associates who manage their 60-plus EPPS events each year are contagious. Lasting and loyal relationships are esteemed and cultivated, and that responsibility resides with everyone, everywhere, at every time. Their team energetically keeps the attendees in each session on schedule by guiding them every step of the way. Charlie Bowlus puts it this way: "If we have a fault we may tend to overcommunicate, but no one seems to be complaining. We contact all attendees to one of our EPPS sessions six weeks in advance and review their schedules and understand what their needs will be on location."

ECRM associates understand the soft needs and the hard needs of all attendees. The hard needs are to meet with 50 or 60 of their trading partners and execute a revenue-producing transaction. The soft needs of every attendee are to feel welcome, significant, included, and informed.

Their business process is facilitated by issuing the latest in tablet computers to all attendees for use in their individual meetings. As you can imagine, this requires careful communication and explicit instructions. Charlie explained that "once attendees arrive on location, one of our account managers meets with them to make certain they are informed, comfortable with the information regarding the schedule, and familiar with the content on their personalized tablet computer. That is just one of four individual contacts a team member has with each attendee at a session."

Efficiency and speed must be assured at every point, making the EPPS experience better than any other in their competitive space.

Charlie pointed out that "buyers and sellers meet for only 15 or 20 minutes in each of the individual private meetings. We make the tracking of information and individual meeting results as streamlined as possible. We want discussion and decisions to be the focus and outcome of the meetings, not administration."

Creating loyalty through differentiation requires continuous improvement. At the conclusion of each EPPS session every attendee (an average of about 350 people per session) meets with an ECRM team member to debrief on all aspects of the session. Feedback is gathered for all facets of the meeting, from location, to scheduling, to the business process, to the event itself, and the social gatherings. Getting better at getting better is what drives ECRM's ongoing success.

Once all of the attendees have departed, the ECRM team meets on location and shares the feedback. Empowerment rules the improvement process, and they have taken a page from Wal-Mart, one of their largest retailer clients, by implementing a process they term *Correction of Errors* (COE). This is their continuous improvement process.

Whoorahs

Internal service and recognition are traits of great service organizations. They encourage the formation and perpetuation of a language of service. ECRM is no exception. One of their service language terms is "Whoorahs." Team members are encouraged to recognize those in the organization who go the extra mile. Their employee Web site has a section where staff members can post messages for one another regarding their achievements. They can be posted by anyone in the organization, from upper-level management to those in entry-level positions. These messages are called "Whoorahs" and can be simple thank you notes for an individual's hard work or support of others, a mention of someone's achievement or growth in a certain area, or even acknowledgment of a special occasion. All team members can view and send these messages daily.

Actual, Real-Life Whoorahs

LESLEY ADAMS SAYS:

> Whooorahhh to Craig . . . for everything you did during Health Week—including keeping your cool when I could not :). THANK YOU!!

CRAIG CHMIELOWICZ SAYS:

> Whoorrahh to Kelly for all her help on the Health Week schedules. You did a great job and saved us days' worth of time.

CRAIG CHMIELOWICZ SAYS:

> Whhooraahh to Lesley for all the time spent on the Health Week schedules and for being on top of everything. You held it all together—could not have done it without you.

KATE BURNS SAYS:

> Whhhoooorah to all of the CSRs for working hard this summer! Thanks to the CSRs in Marco who helped train all of the newbies!

KATE BURNS SAYS:

> Whoooorahhhh to all of the teams and every department! The hectic summer schedule is over :).

A Final Thought

Seeking opportunities to create memories, understanding client needs, seeking continuous improvement, empowerment, and a devotion to the client experience are all traits of ECRM that illustrate *how* they do what they do.

In 1994, ECRM was formed by two people, who had planned two meetings, had a handful of clients, and had a vision. From their inception, the culture of this fine service company was created by Charlie Bowlus.

By 2007 ECRM had grown to be a company of almost 200 people who conduct more than 60 meetings worldwide and serve in excess of 3,000 clients. From their earliest years of holding a few annual events, they reflect on having hosted more than 300 sessions since they first began. More than 700 buyers representing most food, drug, and mass merchandise chains in the United States and a growing number of multinationals from Europe, Asia, and South America participate in sessions each year, as do more than 1,800 consumer packaged goods manufacturers. Loyalty through differentiation is the outcome everyone desires.

How you do what you do is a path to follow.

• The Henry & Horne Story •

What They Do

Henry & Horne, LLP, is one of the largest public accounting and consulting firms in Arizona. They have three offices located throughout the state, each of which operates as a local firm within its own geography. This enables Henry & Horne to cater to individual client needs by providing the personal attention of a local team, backed by the size, strength, resources, and technology of a regional firm.

With more than 50 years of experience representing companies of all types and sizes, Henry & Horne's expertise in accounting principles, tax law, and personal consulting is beyond reproach. Henry & Horne believes strongly that an audit is not a commodity to be awarded to the lowest bidder. They are proud of their reputation as a firm that offers exceptional audit skills, enmeshed with superior personal service—hence, their desire is to serve clients who are not solely concerned with tax code compliance but are seeking a business partner who informs, consults, and advises.

One of the primary reasons Henry & Horne is held in such high esteem is their people. The cliché of bespectacled, introverted CPAs does not apply here; these teams break the mold. Henry & Horne prides itself on finding and retaining people who will work together, serve together, and stay together. The culture of the firm is collegial, collaborative, and confident. They recruit professionals with top-notch skills, but they hire only those who exhibit the qualities of being a team player, a positive attitude, respect for others, and a willingness to go the extra mile for teammates and clients alike. In other words, they *hire for attitude*.

Relationships form the backbone of Henry & Horne's business, and they are a key ingredient of their success. They believe in personalized service, preferring face-to-face contact with their clients over detached electronic communications; but they also make full use of the latest technology as appropriate. They feel most productive when their culture and values mesh with those of their clients—a perspective clearly shared by their clients as evidenced by their satisfaction, loyalty, and tenured relationships.

Henry & Horne has developed a strong and loyal client base, in part because of their exemplary reputation as outstanding accountants and business partners in the financial services industry. But they have nurtured and maintained that following by how well they serve their clients.

Henry & Horne's profile is amazing. Throughout these many chapters, we have stressed the importance of internal service. At Henry & Horne, the manner in which employees serve one another is at the crux of *how* they do what they do. The focus each individual places on one another (internal service) converts to a powerful experience for their clients (external service). If you need further validation of the role behaviors play in service relationships, both inside and outside a company, read this profile carefully.

Henry & Horne's Purpose

> We shall be recognized as the trusted provider of innovative
> fiscal services and information management for the financial
> life cycle of our clients.

Henry & Horne's Purpose is, and always has been, to be a company
built and dependent upon the satisfaction of their clients and associates. Bonded by integrity, trust, a sense of community, flexibility for
accommodating change, and a commitment to long-term relationships, Henry & Horne and their constituents support that Purpose.

Henry & Horne's Values

- Encourage team members to reach their full potential
- Offer encouragement and a firm culture of support
- Develop skills and friendships
- Develop values to guide team members' actions and provide
  the foundation for sound decision making
- Work hard with enthusiasm
- Respect opinions and thoughts of others
- Maintain integrity of the process

Henry & Horne's Culture

Henry & Horne's Purpose and Values reflect the beliefs of their
founding partners. They are at the core of their tradition of Service
Excellence, which has endured the test of time. In our previous
profile of Charlie Bowlus and ECRM, we discussed the importance
Charlie places on the absolute satisfaction of his clients. So it was
with Marvin Henry and Gail Horne when they merged accounting
practices in 1957, creating Henry & Horne CPAs.

Marv Henry is fondly remembered as a down-to-earth, easygoing,
and visionary professional. Gail Horne describes his role in the
firm as "benevolent dictator," while others attribute the company's
position at the forefront of accounting technology to his foresight
and approach to learning and leadership. Both held ardent beliefs

about Service Excellence, which remain at the heart of their culture today.

Fifty years ago, Marv and Gail began with 12 employees working in three locations throughout the state. Together, they built the firm's reputation as a solid, locally owned and operated accounting practice that focused on understanding and satisfying the needs of their clients. Technology revolutionized accounting practices, transforming hand-posted general ledgers into terabytes of data in cyberspace. But despite this changing business landscape, Henry & Horne remained steadfast in their fundamental approach to serving clients.

Mark Eberle, a managing partner, is now the "torch bearer" of Henry & Horne's culture. He explains it this way: "Culture starts at the top, but everyone is responsible for maintaining it. Everyone gets to enjoy the culture, and accordingly, everyone needs to make an effort every day to keep the culture strong and make it better. If someone's not happy, we'll do everything we can to change that. Enjoying one's work experience is a must."

He continued, "When our people are happy and feel good about what they do, this comes through to the clients. It begins with the people we hire. We make sure that the people we hire are nice, caring people who will support and fit in with the culture.

"Celebrating our firm's fiftieth anniversary is more akin to a golden wedding anniversary than perhaps a typical business milestone. It's personal, it's local, and it's a time for reflection. Being surrounded by the friends and family who have grown with us in Arizona since 1957 is what makes us most happy."

Mark's view of this important company milestone is more a salute to their long-term client relationships than it is to Henry & Horne. Their anniversary is a celebration of the clients with whom they have "grown up." From the beginning, their goal has been to provide the best, most personal client service on a local level. Over the past five decades, the nature of their clients' businesses may have changed, but their Purpose and Values remain rock solid. Henry & Horne still takes great pride in serving clients better and better with each passing year.

Traits and Characteristics

We dedicated Chapter 9 to the topic of service traits, and we emphasized the impact of behaviors and attitudes on Service Excellence. This attentiveness to service traits is a hallmark of Henry & Horne; they know it, and clients experience it. They believe clients care deeply about the personal traits of the individuals in their firm and the consequent collective traits of the company. These characteristics have driven their growth and sustainability these past 50 years.

Chuck Inderieden, the partner-in-charge of Henry & Horne's Scottsdale office, feels strongly that the traits and behaviors possessed by each individual have contributed to the growth and evolution of their culture. In his words, "I do not suggest that everyone works in the same precise way but rather that each individual is an individual. Overall they are very pleasant to deal with and care deeply about their clients."

The following are traits that Chuck feels are of greatest importance in serving clients:

- *Being responsive.* Clients like confirmation that their request was heard or read—so I believe the faster one responds, the happier the client.
- *Being proactive.* Clients do not like it when they hear or read about something we should have told them earlier—we need to inform clients about new opportunities, not vice versa.
- *Asking for help.* Don't be afraid to get outside help. We cannot do it all, and we are not experts in all fields of accounting. However, we do have contacts that can help our clients achieve some of their goals better than we can. We are not embarrassed and do not feel weak when we refer them

to others outside the firm. In fact, we only become better providers because we are putting our clients' interests first.

- *Demonstrating you care.* You have to care about your client's problems and issues, and you cannot fake that. The client will know based upon your energy and commitment that you care and worry about their issues.
- *Being knowledgeable.* Knowledge is power in the accounting business. You must be able to sit at a conference room table and demonstrate ideas and suggestions that give value to your client. That means you must go the extra mile to ensure you are completely current in all aspects of the relationship.
- *Demonstrating that team matters.* In a firm our size, it's just too big for one person to do it all. You must have a team to back one another up. Having a strong team and other professionals a client can contact demonstrates that everyone supports the client.

Mark Eberle sums it up this way: "We have attitude indicators. Attitude is everything. Attitude comes first. We simply will not hire anyone with a bad attitude (to life or anything else) regardless of what they might have in talents. A bad attitude drags down the office and rolls over to serving the client. We'll bend over backward to help people who are slipping with their attitudes and help them turn their attitudes back around. However, at the end of the day, a person with a negative attitude or consistent lack of common courtesies won't last at Henry & Horne."

At Henry & Horne, you are exhibiting a good attitude when you

- Do the things that are "not much fun"—which are a part of every job—with a smile and an upbeat attitude.
- Enthusiastically attend and participate in firm-sponsored events (mixers, team meetings, civic functions, and so on).
- Are quick to take responsibility for an error or mistake. Apologize first. Take the high road.
- Are pleasant and upbeat, especially during stressful or difficult times.

- Understand that communication is a never-ending process. You always seek to understand the other party first, and you make repeated and consistent efforts to be sure you are clearly understood.
- Hold yourself accountable for completing assignments and tasks once you accept them, rather than letting them die on the vine without an explanation of why.
- Take pride in your professional dress. A sharp appearance indicates a sharp mind.
- Genuinely help others by pitching in whenever you see someone in need.
- Take responsibility for problems you encounter by addressing the issue with the individual or individuals who can resolve the problem rather than complaining among your team members.
- Meet or exceed internal deadlines. And when you are not able to meet original deadlines, renegotiate the deadline and communicate the reasons behind the delay.
- Set a standard for returning phone calls and e-mail within 24 hours, even if only to tell the caller or e-mailer you'd like to schedule another time to talk.
- Apply the golden rule: treat everyone with respect, regardless of title or seniority, and in the same way you would like to be treated.
- Keep your work area neat, organized, and clean.
- Keep any strong emotions under control, and consider the result of your anger or temper before exhibiting it.
- Get to know the others in your office and show an interest in understanding what they do and how their work interacts with yours.

Mark continued, "We're professionals. We are nice. We care. We exercise common courtesies all day, every day, which is a way of life. All of these characteristics roll over as to how we work with our clients. It's not an act; it's a way of being. We constantly talk about doing the right things the right way—all the time. Keeping commitments and promises, communicating glitches and hurdles as soon as possible—those are proactive traits we all live by.

"We try to avoid the 'hope' that something will work out. We strive to address and discuss issues as soon as possible. We want to understand the clients' needs and what is important to them. If there's a difference of understanding, we work toward common ground whenever possible. We all contribute to growing our culture and work hard to have our people feel good about what they do and where they work. Our people are happy. When our people are happy and feel good about what they do, this comes through to the clients."

As you can tell, Mark is very passionate in his beliefs! And why not? They have been at the heart of Henry & Horne's success.

One of the Best Places to Work

In its fourth year of ranking local companies, the *Phoenix Business Journal* again recognized Henry & Horne as one of the city's Best Places to Work. Henry & Horne was also honored as one of only five companies to have made this list each and every year. This recognition is a proof statement of what companies can achieve when they provide great internal service. People, not numbers, are the most important part of the equation. That is their tagline, and the sentiment extends to their employees and clients alike.

"Henry & Horne strives to make our firm a great place to work," observed Connie Harmsen, firm administrator. "From our comprehensive benefits and compensation packages to our professional development opportunities, we are committed to bettering ourselves and constantly improving the benefits we offer." They clearly care about their internal associates, manifested in their actions (behaviors), not just in their words. The following are some examples of *how* they do what they do:

- The firm holds bimonthly team meetings to share information and news within the firm and to recognize people for significant contributions.
- Each partner has his or her own way of showing appreciation; many give team members tickets to games or gift cards, or they take team members out to lunch.

- The firm provides tax season lunches for everyone, three times a week. They settled on three because they found one day's order generated plenty of leftovers for the next day (in other words, it actually equaled six days' worth of food).
- The administration group of the firm prepares and serves a lunch to their team members each tax season, as a way of saying thank you.
- During tax season, the company provides back massages to all team members.
- The partners host a "Halfway There" party to celebrate that the end of tax season is in sight and to show their appreciation for all the hard work.
- The firm hosts a party at the end of tax season as a way of thanking everyone for their hard work during this stressful time of year.

Connie continued with one more example of Henry & Horne's commitment to internal Service Excellence. "You may have noticed from the preceding list of actions that we use the term 'team members' instead of 'employees' or 'staff.' It says more about the culture of our firm; we believe in being a team and working together. Our receptionist holds the title 'director of first impressions' because this is the first person people meet when they walk through our doors. It's an important job, and we want to recognize its significance with the proper title."

Why is this so important? The next time you contact someone who is serving you, reflect on your first impression. Did you encounter a voice-mail greeting, with computerized instructions for dialing your intended party? Were you forced to use a phone in their lobby and consult a list of names and extensions posted on the wall? Did you have to pass inspection from a uniformed guard before being provided access? What first impression of the company did your experience create?

Internal Service

Henry & Horne prides itself on personal relationships. At each of their offices you are greeted in person, and a "live" person answers all of their incoming phone calls. Remember the soft needs that this level of personal attention satisfies? You feel comfortable, at home, welcomed, and, perhaps best of all, important.

Reflect on this for a moment: Without great internal service, can you ever really achieve external Service Excellence? Consider the service decline in the airline industry. Beset with staggering financial challenges, some airlines requested salary givebacks from their employees. Flight attendants (the directors of first impressions) were particularly hard hit. How frequently have you observed an overwhelming desire on their part to serve passengers? Good service interactions still occur, but today they are the exception, not the rule.

In order to serve external clients well, you must be served well internally. Henry & Horne understands this.

Roles and Training

At Henry & Horne, every team member has a role in, and correspond-ing set of responsibilities for, each of their client relationships. Specific individuals or teams may own the relationship, but every-one in the firm who touches the client has a role to play. Their goal is for a minimum of two people to have detailed knowledge of each client and be accountable for their daily oversight. But whenever a client calls, Henry & Horne strives to have every person with whom they may come in contact be conversant in their business.

Henry & Horne invests in their team members' development via formal training programs. They currently utilize 13 modules that tar-get various aspects of the client relationship, including client rap-port, managing expectations, conflict resolution, and problem solv-ing. Clearly, they realize there is more to the client relationship than *what* they do. This is interesting; they feel they are in the business of asking questions, not just giving answers.

Rainmaking

Henry & Horne hires accountants who possess the knowledge and skills necessary to perform the technical aspects of the job (*what*).

However, developing productive relationships with existing and prospective clients is often a skill beyond an accountant's training and experience. In response, the firm has adopted "Rainmaking" programs to teach the why, when, and how of cultivating beneficial and loyal relationships with clients.

How do you acquire this skill? Henry & Horne believes that Rainmaking is not an innate talent for most people; it is an acquired skill that must be taught, learned, and practiced. Relationship management requires the intersection of knowledge and action; those who simply reflect on information and ponder concepts are doomed to fail. Interaction and personal contact are absolutes.

Rainmaking classes present potential client issues, for which they brainstorm solutions around skills such as listening, serving, and managing expectations. These approaches are reinforced through "lunch-and-learn" sessions, in refresher classes, and at team and office meetings.

Clients matter at Henry & Horne, but so do team members. This is reinforced every day in every aspect of *how* they do what they do.

How they do what they do has determined who they have become.

• The TBWA\Worldwide Story •

Who They Are

TBWA was founded in Paris, France, in 1970. Chiat\Day was founded in Los Angeles, California, in 1968. In 1995, the two agencies merged to fulfill a mutual goal of forming the foremost creative network in the world. Today, TBWA\Worldwide is one of the fastest growing of the top 10 agency networks, with 258 agencies in 75 countries, and more than 10,000 employees worldwide. TBWA\Worldwide (TBWA) serves such iconic brands as Absolut Vodka, adidas, Apple,

Beiersdorf, Energizer, Infiniti, McDonald's, Mars, Michelin, Nissan, Samsonite, and Singapore Airlines.

Clients come to TBWA for its expertise in all facets of brand positioning, launching, and long-term management, including brand strategy development, account management and brand stewardship, new product development, integrated general communications (consumer and B2B), regional marketing, shopper activation, and branded content. In today's world of media proliferation, fragmentation, and convergence, clients benefit from TBWA's leadership at a brand strategy level, as well as its stewardship of all marketing communication activities. And clients stay at TBWA because of how the agency serves their soft needs.

What They Do

Each agency in the TBWA network is grounded in a discipline and mindset called "Disruption" that provides a framework for interrogating and overturning the conventions that may be preventing a brand or company from succeeding. United by this common methodology and strategic vocabulary, TBWA's network of agencies is governed by shared values and intelligence rather than the institutional hierarchy popular with many other networks.

Today's primary challenges for clients are improving return on investment, understanding the optimal mix of marketing media expenditures, and driving better integration of all activities. While many in the marketing and communications industry believe that integration results from the enforcement of strict brand guidelines and continuous coordination between disciplines, TBWA believes that type of orientation yields little more than uniformity at a superficial level—the equivalent of "matching luggage." Armed with this knowledge, TBWA deploys Disruption to help galvanize diverse stakeholders in a focused and collaborative conversation in an effort to develop the biggest, sharpest, most fertile brand idea that will, in turn, inform what the brand believes and how the brand behaves and communicates.

This is an important differentiation in the TBWA approach. Disruption helps the agency network develop a creative strategy that will drive the brand's overarching global success without sacrificing local relevance. And because of the interrogatory nature of the Disruption process, client workshops deter "consensus by committee" or ideas borne of the lowest common denominator.

And yet defining the Disruptive strategy is only half of the equation. The other half is to make sure the agency crafts an idea from the right perspective and then engages the right disciplines to make full use of the media arts landscape.

Whereas media used to be nothing more than a way for brands to target consumers, today media is THE way people are engaging with the world around them—so much so that TBWA defines *media* as "any space between a brand and the audience"—the places, spaces, and experiences in which people choose to spend their time. Consider that Apple stores are now media experiences, and iTunes, in serving millions of songs, podcasts, and playlists, is now the brand delivering the media.

TBWA refers to this as the "Era of Media Arts."

Every agency in the TBWA network is fluent in Disruption and Media Arts. Everyone has led and attended Disruption workshops. Everyone uses the same tools. Collectively, everyone is constantly evaluating and documenting shifts in the media landscape, and the impact of these shifts on audience behavior. The commitment to and practice of these disciplines is what enables TBWA to serve global brands differently from the way their competitors do.

TBWA\Worldwide's Philosophy

TBWA follows two practices that differentiate itself from the competition: Media Arts and Disruption.

Media Arts defines the way the agency connects audiences to a brand's or a company's disruptive idea. Media Arts capitalizes on today's ever-evolving media landscape, using every Connection point from advertising to architecture to social networks to packaging so as to align audiences with contextually creative messages and experiences.

Disruption is a proprietary tool and methodology utilized by TBWA to help companies and brands systematically challenge market conventions, identify new growth opportunities, and develop strategies to drive future success. The practice of Disruption combines the use of over 70 tools and diagnostics on a day-to-day basis, supplemented by collaborative workshops called "Disruption Days." Disruption is part of TBWA's DNA, and as its application has continued to evolve, this discipline has originated consulting businesses in many markets.

Disruption Forms Relationships

Disruption is a tool for change and an agent of growth; and it is a working methodology and a life view philosophy. The word may conjure a sense of discomfort for some, but Disruption is not destructive. It is creative. Disruption is a means of creating something dynamic to replace something that has become static.

Disruption is the art of asking better questions, challenging conventional wisdom, and overturning assumptions and prejudices that impede the imagination of new possibilities and visionary ideas. It is a system for people who hate systems. Disruption has evolved and matured as communities within the TBWA network have used, adapted, and reinvented the tools for specific market or client needs.

The methodology and process can be employed universally to answer just about any challenge a brand or company may encounter. Disruption is not limited to marketing and communications; rather, it can be applied to deeper levels of an organization including products and services or the core business offering.

It is through the process of Disruption that the initial client relationships are formed that become the bridge as the Connections with clients evolve.

TBWA\Worldwide's Culture

Tom Carroll, president and CEO of TBWA\Worldwide, commented on how TBWA differentiates itself from the competition: "The success of the network was not a sure thing when it was put together. In fact, when you look back over the past 30 years, particularly in the United States, the industry is littered with failure. Many big, powerful, and great creative agencies no longer exist. Equally poor outcomes came of the hundreds of mergers and acquisitions—couplings that never delivered on the promise of their combined talent or client rosters."

He continued, "So what is it about a network that brought together TBWA, Chiat\Day, BDDP, and Hunt\Lascaris that defied the odds and succeeded? In our case, these four agencies all shared similar philosophies and a vision for the business. Each had a passion and dedication to creativity—across every department, particularly media. And long before any of us called it 'Disruption,' we each had demonstrated a need to seriously challenge the status quo.

"So it is our culture that separates us from the rest of the world, and I believe it has contributed to our rapid arrival among the top global agency networks. What took our competitors 100 years to accomplish, we did in less than 30. Not only did we catch up, but we are now passing them in terms of growth, global clients, and creativity."

Jean-Marie Dru is chairman of TBWA\Worldwide. In 2007, he published the book *How Disruption Brought Order—The Story of a Winning Strategy in the World of Advertising* in which he discusses the importance of culture in the success of a company. Part memoir, part business playbook, *How Disruption Brought Order* tells the story of what happens behind the scenes when everyone practices the art of Disruption in their own business. It is the story of how TBWA has come to be one of the most successful and creative networks in the world, in an exceptionally short period of time.

Jean-Marie outlines many reasons for this success, but it is clear that the most important is culture. He writes, "Any culture, corporate or not, is the fruit of a collective adventure. Something shared. A mental structure, an evolving language, a collection of desires, a kind of élan, and while culture is legitimized over time, its infancy is equally important."

Communications and Feedback

TBWA facilitates workshops in which client and agency associates engage in a series of exercises designed to explore a specific issue. Highly collaborative, strategic, and creative in nature, these workshops generate actionable output. Using a selection of tools from a bank of over 50 diagnostics, the workshop participants explore three distinct domains necessary for success: Convention, Vision, and of course, Disruption.

Conventions are the limits (either real or perceived) to which organizations often unknowingly adhere: aspects of communication, consumers, the marketplace, and the company that have always "been done that way." By identifying existing conventions and asking why things are the way they are, conventional thinking can be overturned to the benefit of the company. Insights or hidden truths can be leveraged to help clients define a fundamentally different vision of the future, one in which they have a greater share and unlimited potential.

The Vision becomes the guiding premise that opens an organization's horizons and changes how it communicates and acts. In many cases, TBWA's clients have strong and future-forward visions, but they haven't been well articulated to employees or consumers. A well-articulated Vision inspires the people behind the brand. It provides a rallying cry that propels the brand into the future. In the words of Lee Clow, TBWA\Worldwide chief creative officer, "A brand is the sum of all its actions. Who it is, what it does, what the world expects of it . . . If the brand is passionate, honest and committed, innovative, and at the same time inspirational, if the brand is true to its history, its passion, and true to itself, the world will love that brand."

Disruption seeks to retire old, low-yielding ideas and launch new, highly profitable ones. A disruptive idea is, quite simply, the best and fastest way to overturn conventions and achieve a Vision. Over the past three years, TBWA has conducted more than 500 Disruption Day workshops for clients and brands around the world, including Apple, Standard Chartered Bank, adidas, Nissan, PlayStation, Pedigree, and Whiskas. Each of these workshops identified opportunities to redefine how these companies operate, what they offer consumers, and how they communicate.

The Disruption process yields higher-quality input and feedback. TBWA believes that Disruption facilitates creativity, inspiration, and the right environment for the agency to perform at its best. In fact, it feels so strongly about the role of Disruption that when approached by clients to participate in an agency review, TBWA will not compete unless the client is willing to participate in Disruption Day as part of the pitch process. Feedback and communications are hallmarks of Service Excellence, and they are clearly inherent in the TBWA process.

Connecting with Clients

Laurie Coots, TBWA\Worldwide chief marketing officer, put it this way: "Doing great work that drives a client's business is the result of an open and collaborative relationship. We are all about connecting with our clients by communicating deeply and thoroughly. Having a process that in itself is interactive, engaging, and stimulating helps us bring out the best in everyone—what is in their heads and what is in their hearts." She continued, "We pride ourselves on understanding and satisfying the 'soft needs' of our clients. We recognize that clients need to be appreciated, feel involved, to participate, be listened to, and to collaborate. We know that client satisfaction is not a result of just filling orders."

In a previous chapter, we discussed the concept of leading those you serve. Laurie pointed out that agencies used to fall into one of two categories in serving clients: either you were a "creative shop," producing breakthrough or award-winning work that was often criticized for not being strategic, or you merely "filled orders," doing what the client asked of you and relying heavily on their briefs for guidance. In the 1980s, the account planning process helped agencies bring consumer insights into the equation. But other than major consolidation and the unbundling of media services, the agency business hasn't changed much over the years—lagging behind professional services innovations in other industries.

Laurie remarked that "Disruption is TBWA's way of leading those we serve, in that we strive to collaboratively take our clients to a better place, to fulfill their ambitions for their brands and their companies. We do this through our creative product, but Disruption is the reason we are able to do it again and again. In fact, we differentiate ourselves not only by what we do but also by *how* we do what we do."

Another noteworthy element of TBWA's service approach is how they activate each new client relationship: "We begin every relationship with a cultural audit. This is best when it can take place in the pitch stage. The objective is to make certain we understand all aspects of the client: their language, their culture, their rhythm, their expectations of us, what matters most to them, and especially their key performance indicators, how they are judged and evaluated. It is a very complete assessment." Laurie went on to explain that, "You can't be successful in a partnership if you don't have the same finish line in mind. If we create solutions for problems that nobody has the incentive to solve, we will disappoint and fail. If we create solutions that are at odds with a client's culture or business model, we will miss opportunities and fuel nothing but frustration. From this initial understanding of needs, we are able to judge how our client service team should be formed and staffed, ensuring a cultural alignment based on shared values and trust. These are the building blocks for a successful and satisfying partnership."

Traits

Tom Carroll, TBWA\Worldwide president, shared these additional thoughts on client relationships: "In providing creative services, we are intellectually honest in that we try to get clients to see what they may not have seen before. Service Excellence to us is about leading and challenging clients and ourselves to strive to be our very best."

He observed that, "Mediocre agencies tend to protect revenue in hand. Great agencies try to grow their clients—and thus their revenues—by looking at all aspects of a brand situation."

We talked about the traits that Tom looks for in his people. "Trust, intelligence, honesty, courage, and being collaborative are all traits we judge to be important. In creative businesses, egos can challenge client relationships. So we have to be certain that our successes are channeled in such a way as to serve our clients' best interests and always guard against the unbecoming trait of arrogance."

Tom reinforced this point by describing the relationship that exists between Lee Clow, their chief creative officer, and Jean-Marie Dru, their chairman: "When these two first got together, Jean-Marie had the idea for Disruption, and Lee created the strategy to market the concept. Humility guided that collaboration."

Tom talked about his role in the agency: "I suppose I'm the chief client interaction person. It's my job to understand what is really going on between the client teams and the principal, to set the tone for the relationship between both of our companies. I have got to be certain we are building trust by communicating effectively and being completely honest with one another. Creating an environment that is honest and open builds loyalty, which is what we all strive for."

Isn't it interesting? What they do wins clients. *How* they do what they do retains them. And that is what this book is all about.

High performance. Delivered.

• The Accenture Story •

What They Do

Accenture is a global management consulting, technology services, and outsourcing company, with net revenues of nearly $20 billion. The company employs approximately 175,000 people in 49 countries. Committed to delivering innovation, Accenture collaborates with its clients to help them become high-performance businesses and governments. Accenture's "high-performance-business strategy" builds on the company's expertise in consulting, technology, and outsourcing to help clients perform at their highest levels so that they can create sustainable value for their customers and shareholders.

Using its industry knowledge, service offering expertise, and technology capabilities, Accenture can identify new business and technology trends and develop solutions to help clients around the world

- Enter new markets.
- Increase revenues in existing markets.
- Improve operational performance.
- Deliver their products and services more effectively and efficiently.

Accenture has extensive relationships with the world's leading companies and governments, and they work with organizations that include 94 of the Fortune Global 100 and more than two-thirds of the Fortune Global 500. The company recognizes that their commitment to client satisfaction strengthens and extends their relationships, and they believe very strongly that *how* they do what they do is one of their defining characteristics and is their identified bridge to differentiation and loyalty. To illustrate this point, in fiscal year 2007 the company's top 100 clients, as measured in revenue, had all been clients for at least five years, and 85 of those had been clients for at least ten years. According to Jill Smart, Accenture's chief human resources officer, these long-term relationships are an affirmation of their clients' appreciation for "*how* they do what they do."

Accenture's wide-ranging capabilities in management consulting, systems integration, and outsourcing are enhanced through their alliances with some of the world's most renowned technology organizations. This gives Accenture the ability to provide their clients with end-to-end transformational services in every part of their business, from strategic planning to day-to-day operations. With deep industry and functional expertise, broad global resources, and a proven track record, Accenture can mobilize the right people, skills, and technologies to help clients improve their performance in virtually any area of their business.

Purpose and Values guide great service companies. Accenture's senior leadership has held to a history of following certain beliefs and supporting consistent client-focused vision and Values.

Accenture's Values

Bill Green, Accenture's current chairman and CEO, eloquently expresses the high value they place on people and their role in creating memorable client experiences: "One of the most important issues on the minds of CEOs today is what I call the 'people agenda.' Most leaders agree that having a skilled, experienced, and engaged workforce is critical for success. They also recognize that achieving the full potential of a workforce is a huge challenge.

"To unleash the value within their workforces, leaders need to make sure that their employees are aligned with strategic goals. Employees must be laser focused on their internal and external customers and motivated to bring both intelligence and intuition to those relationships. And they must be flexible and able to adjust, as needed, to continually improve the customer experience. All of this requires leaders who not only attract, retain, and invest in the right people but also educate, energize, and inspire them."

Accenture's six core Values have shaped the culture and defined the character of the company, guiding employee behavior and decision making. In the company's own words, these Values are the following:

- *Stewardship.* Building a heritage for future generations, acting with an owner mentality, developing people everywhere we are, and meeting our commitments to all internal and external stakeholders
- *Best people.* Attracting and developing the best talent for our business, stretching our people, and developing a can-do attitude
- *Client value creation.* Improving our clients' business performance, creating long-term, win-win relationships, and focusing on execution excellence
- *One global network.* Mobilizing the power of teaming to deliver consistently exceptional service to our clients anywhere in the world
- *Respect for the individual.* Valuing diversity, ensuring an interesting and inclusive environment, and treating people as we would like to be treated ourselves
- *Integrity.* Inspiring trust by taking responsibility, acting ethically, and encouraging honest and open debate

In a conversation with Jill Smart, she shared her views about how the company's Values affect her personally: "I have been with Accenture for 27 years, and it is our culture that keeps me here. Our culture is truly shaped and defined by our Values. These are not just words; our Values permeate all we do because our people live them every day."

She continued with an illustration: "You just mentioned Stewardship, which is about building a better future for the next generation of people. Every day, our leaders make decisions on the basis of what is best for our clients and their futures, not just about what is best for Accenture. Their decisions are not based on what is the best thing for them as an individual. Their decisions are based on what is best for our clients and, therefore, for Accenture. This is an example of living our Values, isn't it?"

Jill's excitement about this topic was palpable as she continued: "Internally, our culture is noncompetitive. Of course we compete in the marketplace, and do so very well, but among us, the focus is on teamwork and collaboration. You will not succeed at Accenture if you cannot work effectively as a team member. Everyone has that owner mentality and, therefore, a stake in the collective success of the company."

High-Performance Businesses

Accenture defines *high-performance businesses* as those that accomplish the following:

- Effectively balance current needs and future opportunities
- Consistently outperform peers in revenue growth, profitability, and total return to shareholders
- Sustain their superiority across time, business cycles, industry disruptions, and changes in leadership

And how do high-performers achieve these feats? The company's research has identified the *how* as the following building blocks of high performance.

Market Focus and Position

Market focus and position are the "where and how to compete" aspects of business strategy. High-performance businesses seek unique insights into drivers of current and future value and anticipate changes and translate them rapidly into differentiated operating models and business architectures. Moreover, they focus continuously on business model and service innovation, making markets rather than just riding them.

Distinctive Capabilities

In addition to concentrating on market position and scale, top performers also focus on mastering distinctive capabilities relevant to their target customers.

Performance Anatomy

If distinctive capabilities can be thought of in terms of functional mastery, performance anatomy is about the organizational characteristics that underpin these capabilities. High-performance businesses unleash the organization's energies and core competencies, accelerate insight into action to out-execute competition, and manage the balance between today and tomorrow. *Performance anatomy* is not just a fancy term for culture. It is determined by the mindset top management brings to such diverse areas as strategy, planning and financial control, leadership and people development, performance management, and use of information technology.

High-performance businesses continually balance, align, and renew the three building blocks of high performance, creating their competitive essence through a careful combination of insight and action.

Performance Anatomy: A Deeper View

During my conversation with Jill, I asked her to expand on Accenture's approach to differentiation. She began by clarifying their commitment to consistency: "Being a truly global company, we have developed an Accenture methodology, in which all of our professionals are well versed. We need to be certain that we are delivering the same experience and taking the same approaches with our clients around the globe."

Competing companies can, for a time, appear almost identical. They may share the same targeted markets, business model, revenue base, and employee compensation levels, among countless other features. But over time, these companies' performances start to vary, and soon it becomes obvious they never really were the same. Where they differ is in something Accenture's research calls "performance anatomy."

Performance anatomy runs deep inside an organization, and it affects all of its employees and functions. Performance anatomy is neither hereditary nor accidental. It is the outcome of deliberate choices made by senior executives. Yet it is also by nature elusive, rarely if ever reducible to a statement of vision and Values.

It represents a unique way of approaching the core elements common to every business: leadership and strategy, people development, technology enablement, performance management, and innovation. In other words, performance anatomy is similar to culture in that it expresses the vision and Values of the organization, especially those of the founders. But it is different in that it contains very clear and explicit directions for how each of those core elements ought to be managed and what competencies the organization needs to develop to achieve high performance.

Performance anatomy represents a distinctive perspective on the interaction and the integration of those core elements; that is, how and why they relate to one another the way they do. High-performance businesses, Accenture argues, actively manage the interaction between leadership and strategy, people development, IT enablement, performance measurement, and innovation in a way that produces outstanding and sustainable results. Conventional treatments of culture provide little insight into how companies manage these interactions; performance anatomy does.

CEOs and their top management teams make integration of those elements a primary responsibility, whether they do it intuitively or programmatically. Indeed, the ability of a top management team to actively build the organization's performance anatomy is testimony to its deep understanding of the competitive essence of the business. Thus, performance anatomy represents more than values and assumptions. It represents a touchstone, guarded and stewarded by the CEO, which aligns the top management team; a touchstone that is absolutely essential in an increasingly turbulent and uncertain business environment.

The impact of performance anatomy is profound. It touches decisions about organization design, business models, incentives and values, and top management team composition and succession; it affects the long-term effectiveness, quality, and speed of decision making, as well as the mastery of change and innovation productivity. But most importantly, it connects people all along the operational continuum.

Bringing It Together: Client Relationships

In serving their clients, Accenture works hard at sorting out the *what* from the *how* in order to differentiate from their competitors. Marco Ziegler, a senior executive, has been involved with many of Accenture's consumer products and retail client teams throughout his career; Best Buy, Barnes & Noble, Kimberly-Clark, and Wrigley are just a few. He talks about Accenture's people and service-centric culture with great passion: "Our people contribute to the client relationship process significantly. In fact, they are the very fabric of its strength," he says. He goes on to describe how the company directs teams locally and globally. "Accountability through collaboration is at the center of how we manage clients globally. The culture of Accenture is the same throughout the world, but we obviously incorporate the culture of the locale."

In discussing the pride Accenture takes in their client performance, he described how the company monitors that through client surveys taken every six months, as well as through quarterly reviews that further examine client satisfaction.

"We have experienced senior consultants whose primary role is to interview clients one to one to evaluate the level of client satisfaction and the state of that relationship," he says. "These certified partners in performance quality are not members of a specific team but rather are independent of a client team's ongoing work." Marco went on to emphasize that 70 to 80 percent of the feedback is about *how* Accenture people do what they do.

We talked about the traits that embody Accenture's individuals and client teams. "Excellence in all we do guides us, and we are ever mindful of our Purpose and Values," he commented. "We are cooperative toward each other, positive in attitude, optimistic and humble in our approach to clients." He further explained, "We are proactive in 'getting things done.'

We consider ourselves a flat organization; thus, if a client has a question or concern that a team can't answer, we will find that answer somewhere in our company post haste."

Differentiation through Service Excellence is an accepted premise within Accenture. The company conducts ongoing training for employees of all levels, from analysts through senior executives, and certifies certain competencies at all levels. Built into every one of their "schools" are the service behaviors the company expects of their client-interacting people. This focus on external client service applies equally to the company's internal service expectations.

Jill quantified Accenture's ardent commitment to training by noting that, "Last year, we spent more than $700 million on formal training programs. Sure, we train our people on *what* we do, but we also put significant resources against the *how.* Accenture's people, culture, and client loyalty are all intertwined.

"Very simply, we are known for helping our clients achieve high performance and for the individuals and teams who make that happen. When clients first hire Accenture, they do so largely because of *what* we do—we deliver high performance. But our client loyalty demonstrates that we are rehired and retained because of *how* we do what we do. And that is a testament to our people."

In earlier chapters, we talked about how Starbucks is known for its coffee but it's their people that make them famous. So it is with Accenture. What a great tribute.

A SUCCESSFUL LEARNING

It was 1968, and I was a young sales manager with Lipton. I had just inherited a district of well-meaning but clichéd salespeople, whose approach to serving clients and customers was unimaginative and a bit musty. I was intent on transforming how they did what they did by encouraging everyone to "Get Involved!" I pushed them to try new approaches, think of new ideas, and offer new solutions. I prodded them to unleash their imaginations, increase our visibility, differentiate ourselves, and serve customers better by hitting new heights.

In those days before e-mail and voice-mail, I would write a weekly "Get Involved" letter for distribution to the entire team, sharing new ideas and examples of the successes that were beginning to surface in our district. Every Thursday, we would mimeograph (you young kids will need to look that up) the success stories letter, and we would mail it to everyone's home for arrival on Saturday morning. I purchased a rubber stamp that said GET INVOLVED in one-inch-high bold lettering. Using a red ink pad, we began stamping each letter to our sales group of 60, encouraging them to GET INVOLVED. That catch phrase on a rubber stamp became our symbol of transformation.

The ideas trickled in gradually at first, but quickly they began building in quantity and quality. By publicly recognizing everyone's ideas and successes, a transformation movement began to unfold in our district. One particularly enthusiastic individual, Don Lord, asked if he could have his own GET INVOLVED stamp for use on his correspondence. Of course I was thrilled with the idea, and with that, our transformation took on a new and expanded dimension. Everyone wanted to be awarded a GET INVOLVED rubber stamp!

Thus began a tidal wave of ideas, solutions, and accomplishments. By year's end, I had awarded nearly every district salesperson his or her very own GET INVOLVED stamp. Not coincidentally, this was also the year our district transformed itself. Sales exceeded all targets, and the district earned a 25 percent bonus, which was the maximum allowed. It was the first time in the district's history they had achieved that level of recognition, and it was also the highest bonus paid anywhere in the country that year.

A simple rubber stamp that urged people to GET INVOLVED and that celebrated their success when doing so was the differentiator.

LESSON TO REMEMBER

An unpretentious idea became a successful approach to encouraging everyone, everywhere to participate in changing *how* they did what they did. That change resulted in success levels never before achieved. So decide what will differentiate you: Will it be Whoorahs, Rainmaking, Disruption, Performance Anatomy, a rubber stamp, or something else? You too can experience similar results. Just decide to change and watch what happens.

14

What Do You Do Next?

It has always perplexed me to hear someone remark that, "We rarely lose a client because of *what* we do on their behalf; invariably, our client relationships are severed because of *how* we do what we do on their behalf." Why does this confound me? Because consider that *what* we do is, by and large, the more challenging aspect of our client engagements. *How* we do what we do is a manifestation of our attitudes and behaviors—over which we have complete control!

As you near the end of the book, our hope is that you have begun the process of honestly assessing the "state of service" in your company or team or in your personal work life. Through our examples and exercises, you most certainly have a better understanding of how well you are serving internal and external clients and of how well you are being served. We have challenged you to consider change. We have demonstrated that by choosing a path of transformation, you will differentiate yourself from those with whom you compete.

At your very core, you know if change is essential to your future success. Should you decide to embark on this journey, this book presents you with a roadmap that will guide your process of change and deliver you to your destination of Service Excellence.

CROSSMARK: A Look Back

My last trip to CROSSMARK headquarters had been in December 2006. Our formal involvement in their cultural transformation had concluded. My role had changed from "quarterback," visibly advancing their awareness of Service Excellence on the field, to "cheerleader," rooting for their success from the sidelines. It was now October 2007, and I was anxiously anticipating my first formal meeting with CROSSMARK in 10 months.

During those intervening months, I had spoken to quite a few of their associates and senior leadership members but never in a formal setting. I'd had the opportunity to casually inquire about the progress of their cultural transformation, and I had received consistently positive feedback. This would be my first occasion to have a structured meeting with their senior Service Leadership team, specifically to discuss the progress of their cultural transformation, degree of shared ownership, and outlook for sustainability.

I was understandably anxious, yet excited, to learn how CROSSMARK was progressing without their "training wheels." During our three-year engagement, we had traveled thousands of miles, met with hundreds of people, and collectively worked through the five steps of our roadmap to Service Excellence:

- They had clearly defined their Purpose.
- They had created a series of Values in support of their Purpose.
- They had learned to understand and differentiate between different need sets.
- They had explored ways in which to satisfy those needs.
- They had developed Service Action Plans to ensure excellence in serving their clients.

CROSSMARK had become an organization focused on achieving Service Excellence. Ownership of the culture was theirs; how were they faring?

Service Leadership

CROSSMARK's original senior Service Leaders were Clay Curtis, Rodger Fisher, and David Peet. The team had since been expanded to include Johnette Oden-Brunson, Steve Randecker, and 8 other associates representing diverse roles and areas of the country. Collectively, they form the nucleus of their Service Steering Committee. This increase from 3 to 13 people added geographic reach and functional depth to the committee, thereby enhancing their effectiveness in guiding the cultural deep-rooting process.

The Service Steering Committee convenes twice a month, for a minimum of two hours. During our meeting that October, the team shared with me some of the guidelines they had implemented to institutionalize this culture of Service Excellence and to lay down deep roots:

- Every CROSSMARK associate, regardless of role or location, is required to attend a one-hour monthly service meeting at his or her local office or a nearby location.
- These service meetings are moderated by the local Service Leaders, of which there are 40 throughout North America.
- The agenda points for these meetings are developed by the Service Steering Committee to ensure consistency, but all agenda items must relate to the service transformation and provide a continued focus on *how* they do what they do.
- The local Service Leaders participate in monthly conference calls with the senior Service Leadership team, again to ensure consistency, communication, and alignment.
- In addition to leading these local service meetings, the local Service Leaders chair local Service Steering Committees to ensure "grassroots deep rooting."

Transformation Support

The Service Steering Committee is also responsible for defining, formulating, and implementing the back-room drivers that will advance and sustain their cultural transformation. At CROSS-MARK, these have taken the form of various hiring, training, evaluation, and recognition practices as follows:

- To ensure that all new hires possess the traits required to support a Service Excellence culture, the committee created service behavior–related questions for use in all interviews and to guide final hiring decisions.
- A "Service 101" training course was developed for new associates. This mandatory program instills in everyone the significance of internal and external service practices.
- Annual performance evaluation metrics were modified to encompass service standards.
- Service-specific communiqués (for example, the bulletin board) were established to recognize and communicate great service actions of individuals throughout the company.
- Service-only recognition programs were established, as was CROSSMARK's highest award, "The Mark of Service Excellence," which is bestowed upon those individuals who have distinguished themselves for Service Excellence practices three times.

What Is Happening?

The evolution of CROSSMARK's cultural transformation is producing interesting and delightful results, both internally among associates and externally with clients. The senior Service Leadership team has noted that their cultural transformation is taking root faster than expected. Everyone everywhere is embracing the culture. In Malcolm Gladwell's vernacular, the "virus of good service" appears to be spreading. The new culture is starting to weed out those associates for whom there is no fit within a Service Excellence environment, whether because of aptitude or attitude. The internal relationships among associates have clearly benefited from CROSSMARK's transformation efforts.

At the outset of our transformation process, many CROSSMARK associates asked, "How will we know when this is working?" Our answer was, "You will feel the difference by how people interact with one another." On this day in October, I witnessed a discernible difference in the atmosphere at CROSSMARK's headquarters; feelings of cooperation and inclusion were pervasive. As we ended our meeting, I noticed close to 500 people having a lively group conversation over lunch with their CEO David Baxley. After the luncheon, David remarked, "This all is coming together; our people feel the difference, and clients are sensing that we are changing. It is all good."

As concrete evidence, during the summer of 2007, CROSSMARK was appointed the exclusive retail partner for the American Express (AmEx) Retail Gift Card, the fastest-growing division within the American Express brand. Thien Truong, AmEx's U.S. vice president of sales for this division, shared their rationale for this appointment in a companywide address to all CROSSMARK associates: "You were chosen as our exclusive retail partner for the simple fact that both our companies share the same attributes of trust, integrity, quality, and superior customer service."

Recall how Dale Brunner of the Four Seasons commented that he lives his life as he lives the Four Seasons' culture? At my October 2007 meeting with the CROSSMARK senior Service Leadership team, David Peet remarked that the "cultural transformation is taking hold faster than we expected. We have gone from being on a journey, to developing into a movement, and now it is becoming our way of life."

This is the taste of success. This is when you know the roots of your new culture are spreading wide and deep. Transformation evolves to sustenance and nourishment. "It is all good." Service Excellence is working for them.

The Rest of the Story

The internal relationships among associates had clearly benefited from CROSSMARK's transformation efforts, but what about the business results that would set this apart from other feel-good initiatives? I asked the senior Service Leadership team for specifics on their performance in the areas of competitive differentiation, client loyalty, and business growth—all areas for improvement identified at the outset. They responded that they were experiencing positive results in each of those areas, as evidenced by the following metrics:

- An uninterrupted trajectory of annual revenue growth
- An expansion of CROSSMARK's client roster
- Continued increases in client satisfaction ratings over the past five years
- Recognition bonuses for CROSSMARK associates in 2007, in acknowledgment of these achievements

So How Difficult Is This?

It is not unusual for my friends, colleagues, and clients to assert, "This entire notion of Service Excellence is so simple and straightforward." Ah, but that raises this question: If Service Excellence is indeed simple, then why is the state of service so dismal, and why do so few individuals and companies serve you well? The answer is that, as we know, achieving Service Excellence is more illusive and challenging than it appears on the surface.

At the heart of Service Excellence is a strong desire to serve others. It is fueled by selfless beliefs, attitudes, and behaviors; by forming emotional connections with those you serve; and by caring for the needs of others and putting those needs first in the pursuit of their ultimate satisfaction. Conveying this in all you do, in every facet of your relationships, and in every interaction, is far from simple.

But it can be achieved. Remember that getting to Service Excellence is a journey, which begins simply with the first step. This book will be your guide; everything you need for your journey is here. When you are ready to embark on your transformation, return to page 51 and take that first step. We guarantee you will never look back. Good luck.

A Final Thought

The choice is yours . . .
You can choose to change, or you can remain as you are.

Differentiation through Service Excellence is a guaranteed bridge to loyalty. We have presented a roadmap to achieve this goal. It works. We have shared the Service Excellence approach of many successful, yet different companies. It works.

However, there is an even larger question everyone must address: "How do you want to be remembered?" Answer this question from both a professional and a personal standpoint. If your answer is, "I want to be defined by *what* I did in life," then your path is clear. If instead your answer is, "I want to be remembered for *how* I did what I did," then your path is different.

You need only decide which path to take and, if necessary, enact the changes to set your plan in motion.

My Opinion?

How you do *what* you do will determine the person you be-come . . . and how you will be remembered.

Afterword

How you do what you do represents what I have learned over a lifetime of providing service to clients and customers in various capacities. It has been a very fulfilling journey marked with many occasions of success and failure, surprise and disappointment, good news and bad news, with each occasion proving to be a learning experience. The valuable insight I gained is what I desired to share with you in this book. Service Excellence is about individuals interacting in a manner that makes all parties feel good about the experience. When we grow as individuals, our relationships grow as well. And if we consistently interact well with those we serve, loyalty results.

My intention is that this book will provide you with a roadmap that can lead you to a personal, team, or companywide transformation. It is an approach that I have seen succeed. This roadmap, coupled with your own beliefs, attitudes, behaviors, and good traits, is what will raise to a level of excellence the experience you create for those you serve.

Most likely, many of your beliefs, attitudes, behaviors, and traits are already formed. If they are, and the resultant experience is satisfying to you and to those you serve, then continue on your journey, pausing only to reflect on how you might improve by adding some pieces of our roadmap. If they are not, then you must begin a complete transformation.

What follows is a summary of the methods that lie at the heart of your transformation roadmap.

- **How important is service in America today?**
  Never has *service* been such a critical factor in securing and maintaining business and personal relationships. With fierce competition for limited client attention and re- sources, service can become a means to competitive differ- entiation through which lasting and enduring success and loyalty can be built and retained for life.

- **Can *you* gain the first adopter advantage?**
  In a competitive business environment, the companies that are first to embrace a positive change in the way they do business are the ones that gain competitive advantage. A service-driven approach can be the pathway to competitive advantage in any business.

- **What is Service Excellence?**
  Service Excellence is less about *what* you do on behalf of the people you are serving and more about *how* you do what you do. It is about making long-term commitments to change your approach to serving. People will measure you by how you behave, *not* by what you say about how you behave.

- **Whom do you serve?**
  You serve everyone—clients, customers, and colleagues. Teamwork is at the center of your service process. The more you serve each other, the better you become as a Service Excellence team or individual.

- **Why embark on a cultural service transformation?**
  You need to differentiate yourself from those with whom you compete. Others may match your price, your product, your process. If you can differentiate yourself by *how you do*

what you do, your competitors will only aspire to match you at service.

- **Long-term loyalty is the priority.**
  Your success as a service-driven company will be determined not only by how you treat those outside of the company but also by how you serve your colleagues inside the company. In a competitive industry, the companies that are *first* to embrace change in the way they do business are the ones that gain competitive advantage. A service-driven approach will lead to competitive advantage.

- **Develop your Purpose.**
  Purpose defines you. It is why you do what you do. In order to be successful, it is first necessary to determine what it is you wish to be successful in doing. Purpose is the drive behind what you do and how you want to do it. It is about how you want to be remembered.

- **Establish your Values.**
  Values are the guidelines that govern your behavior. When your Values are right, your behaviors will be right. Values come in three forms: business, personal, and ethical.

- **What are the elements of a great service relationship?**
  You must genuinely care about the people you serve.

  You must fully understand and be willing to satisfy their needs.

  You must communicate frequently, honestly, and openly.

  You must put the needs of others first.

- **Understand client needs.**
  Everyone has two sets of needs: hard needs and soft needs.

  Hard needs are satisfied by the work (what) you do on someone's behalf. This satisfaction comes to someone you

serve by your doing what you do really well. Satisfying
hard needs creates a feeling that you have done your job
successfully. Hard needs are fundamental. All your competitors satisfy them as well.

Soft needs are satisfied by *how* you do your work (your
behavior). Soft needs reside in all of us. They are more difficult to uncover and are by their nature more significant,
because satisfying soft needs requires an emotional connection with and deeper understanding of the people you are
serving. Satisfying soft needs will provide a unique point of
differentiation. Awareness, probing discussions, and sensitivity are the keys to your success in satisfying these needs.

- **Satisfy client needs.**
  Do the common thing in an uncommon way; make the
  ordinary seem extraordinary; look at the routine and make
  it special; use your imagination; be open to spontaneity in
  your service actions; take risks.

  Seek opportunities to create memories, because there are
  no expiration dates on memories.

  Stay in all of your service moments so that you are keenly
  aware of what is occurring. Your challenge is to find those
  opportunities that allow you to differentiate yourself from
  the competition and to reinforce to the people you are
  serving just how important they are.

  Give more than you promise rather than promising more
  than you can give.

  Give those you serve more than they expect: surprise . . .
  surprise . . . surprise.

- **Trust matters.**
  Trust is a confident dependence on the character, ability, or
  truth of someone or something. If you serve well, you will
  be respected, valued, and trusted. You become a significant
  resource, a reliable partner, and a loyal supplier. Remem-

ber, trust is always yours to retain, build, or, sadly, lose. Trust is about personal integrity.

- **Secure feedback by asking those you serve: Tell me three things you like about how I serve you. Tell me three things I should improve.**
  Feedback is the key to great service. However it isn't feedback if you don't listen. You must believe the feedback you are given. Don't be defensive; welcome an opportunity to improve. Don't make excuses.

- **Create your written Service Action Plans.**
  Your Service Action Plans are never static. They must evolve. What constituencies/individuals are the focus of your Service Action Plans? Have you listed service actions with time-bound plans? Are you adding a creative service action to your action plans?

- **Embrace traits of great people you admire.**
  Recognize the differences between skill, attitude, and behavior.

  When your attitudes are right, your behaviors will be as well. You must achieve this by constantly monitoring your behavior.

- **Continue to seek improvement.**
  The only goal to shoot for when it comes to an acceptable performance level is 100 percent (perfection). The only way you can approach perfection is through feedback and measurement. You probably will never achieve perfection, but in striving for it, you can realize excellence. Getting better at getting better is the goal of continuous improvement.

- **Personal traits are what define who you really are.**
  The desire to serve is a basic trait for excellent service people.

Humility and great service seem to go hand in hand.
Being proactive is an admirable trait.

- *How* **you do what you do will determine who you will become.**
  This sentence captures the very essence of what your cultural service transformation is all about. *How* you serve those you serve will determine the ultimate success you achieve in your quest to reach Service Excellence.

These summary points are at the center of your personal, team, or company transformation. This approach works. It is simple, complete, and connected. It is habit-forming if understood, embraced, and practiced continually. The complete roadmap is provided. Follow it and you will succeed.

How You Do . . . What You Do is dedicated to excellent service people everywhere. I hope that after reading this book there will be many more of you out there. Thank you for taking the time, and I hope you enjoyed the experience.

Acknowledgments

In June 1960, I began a magnificent journey in the form of a career that introduced and linked me to thousands of people engaged in the business of serving customers and clients. When this book is published, I will have spent nearly 50 years in this special profession. In some ways, it seems like only yesterday that I interviewed for my first job with Cliff Boxer, an assistant district manager at the Campbell Soup Company. I wore a borrowed suit and, as was customary in those days, a summer straw hat.

Upon reflection, I don't believe I was answering a special call to make "service" my life's work; I believe it simply unfolded that way. Early on, I realized that this would be a career of incredible highs and lows, anxieties and frustrations, disappointments and happiness—competing emotions that could actually occur simultaneously! Many years later, it became clear that the pleasure and satisfaction I derived from my work was directly proportional to the pleasure and satisfaction experienced by those I served.

While pursuing this long career of serving others, I envisioned that one day I would share the path to service success that I had learned, practiced, refined, tested, and taught over the years. For those individuals and companies who are deeply committed to serving well and who consider all service professions to be splendid and noble, I offer this book.

I would like to take this opportunity to recognize certain people and companies who have had a profound impact on me both personally and professionally in countless ways throughout my journey.

In preparing to write this book, there was a four-year span that gave me the rare opportunity to work with my son Rob. He was a major contributor to the successful service transformation we worked on together at CROSSMARK. Most of the material that makes up this book was created and fine-tuned while we were working together. Some of the research and support information came from his experience and knowledge. As I've said several times to the people of CROSSMARK, we were so appreciative of the opportunity given us to validate our service beliefs based on a lifetime's work. In addition, having the opportunity to work with your son is an experience every father should have. Thanks, Rob.

As the writing of this book unfolded, two people assisted me significantly throughout all steps of the process. Without them, I would still be plugging away on my PC.

Maureen McGlynn, a great service person in her own right, brought many of these words and thoughts "to bright" through her gifted writing skills, coupled with her true understanding of how you do what you do. "Punching up" was the expression she used laughingly; excellence in writing composition and editing would be my terminology. She truly loves writing, and it shows throughout this book. Thank you, Maureen.

Jonathan Olson, a recent graduate of the University of Southern California, was a significant research resource, and his work was a validation of the approach as understood by one of tomorrow's business leaders. He was a terrific sounding board, and he researched information thoroughly and carefully. Jon has a marvelous career ahead of him, and any of you readers looking for a young genius should hire him (jon.douglas.olson@gmail.com).

Tom Markert, CEO of IPSOS Loyalty and a two-time published author, was someone I have mentored for years. Tom became *my* mentor in the early stages of securing a publisher and framing my thoughts into a book, and he helped me enormously.

Finally and notably, some of the wonderful people at McGraw-Hill: Knox Huston was my fabulous editor who took me on as an inexperienced first-time author and guided me through the writing and publishing process. He was patient, always there for me, and indeed a great Service Excellence person. Herb Schaffner, group publisher for business, was supportive throughout the entire publishing process. Jane Palmieri, editing manager, came in near the end and without her this book would not read nearly as well as it does.

A special thank you to Ben Manibog and Tiffany Chan, who assisted with the cover design. Thank you also to Dan Lueders and Brad Braun, my reliable attorneys.

A major salute goes to Jim Borders who is now retired from CROSSMARK but who was, during their culture transformation, their COO. He rode every airplane and attended every meeting we put on for them. His leadership and support were deeply appreciated.

Thank you to the many people who read the various stages of manuscripts developed throughout the writing process: John Lewis, my very special and gifted friend; Danny Sacco, my great pal and alter ego; Kathy Rasmussen; Rich Collins; Rich Maryyanek; Ron Douglas; Phil Lempert; Paul Bello; Bill Graham; Bruce Graber; Nick D'Agostino; Phil McGrath; Kate Conklin; Victor Hailey; Lisa Miller; Alex Siskos; Karen Fichuk; Betsy Komjathy; Dave Pinto; Margaret Ross; Anastasia Mann; Gus Alfieri; John Caron; and Duncan Mac Naughton. To the fabulous team at FedEx Kinko's on Sunset who printed all the manuscripts.

Thank you to everyone at CROSSMARK for their cooperation, belief, and support of REL Communications and for their unwavering commitment to Service Excellence: David Baxley, Joe Crafton, Ben Fischer, Don Martin, David Peet, Rodger Fisher, Clay Curtis, Steve Randecker, Johnette Oden-Brunson, and Bill

Sheffer. Thank you to Stephanie Patrick, Hubert Bitner, James Miller, Mike Permenter, and Stephanie Scott for all of their assistance throughout our three-year assignment. A special thank you goes to John Thompson who has been there since this project began and is still leading the charge.

Thank you to the people of The Nielsen Company, especially David Calhoun for writing the foreword, Kyle Schauenberg, Stacey Gallagher, Debbie Hoyt, Jon Mandel, Terry Morrissey, Mitchell Habib, Kathie Miller, Mary Jo Mendell, Judy Anderson, Dirk Izzo, Cheryl Pearson-McNeil, and Jack Loftus. Thank you to Howard Gross and Daniel Delson of Robinson Lerer & Montgomery for their sound advice and guidance.

Thank you also to Chris Allieri, Jill Kouri, Stacey Jones, Jill B. Smart, and Marco Ziegler of Accenture; Chuck Inderieden, Mark Eberle, and Jaime Czarneski of Henry & Horne; Charlie Bowlus of ECRM; and TBWA\Worldwide, specifically Lisa Reddig, Laurie Coots, Tom Carroll, and Jeremy Miller, all of whom contributed great insight to their company profiles.

To all my friends at the Four Seasons, a thank you, especially to Mehdi Eftekari, Carol Watkins, Ephrem, Sarah Cairns, Dale Brunner, and Dana Bronson.

To Brad Paisley, Brent Long, Doug Paisley, and the "road gang": you are all terrific.

Dabney Bixel is a role model when it comes to Service Excellence. Her encouragement to write this book and her support throughout kept me on schedule. Thanks to Robert and Jonathan, terrific brothers and friends; Elle, a beautiful English springer spaniel who sat at my side throughout; thank you all.

One of the great "second career" joys that can come to someone is the mentoring you are able to do. From those I mentored came reinforced knowledge that keeps me current as I evolve in this "Corporate Witness Relocation Program" phase of life; you know who you are. To Gary Doyle, Pete Deeb, Frank Cleveland,

Tom Aquilina, Bill Kies, and Henry Johnson, my sometimes REL and consulting colleagues: thanks, guys, for those years together.

To every one of my Lipton colleagues and friends, far too extensive in number to list but ever so significant because of what they contributed to their families, clients, customers, company, and my life as I reflect back on those many years we all served together. You were very special people in very special times, and we should never forget those. How you all did what you did taught me a great deal.

A noteworthy thank you must go to all of the clients and customers I have served throughout my career. Through your support, patience, cooperation, suggestions, and help, you taught me how to do what I did. Here again the list of the individual people and companies would fill a chapter. I thank you and appreciate all of you.

Last but most important, a special thank you goes to my very bright and wonderful daughter Susan; my son-in-law Tom Van Buskirk; my grandchildren Andrew, Caroline, and Katie Van Buskirk and Joan Livingston; and my sister Barbara Ivory. You all witnessed a lot of what I wrote about throughout.

A GRATEFUL LEARNING

When you sell, you always end a conversation by saying *thank you* to them.

When you serve someone else well, the person being served says *thank you* to you.

I say thank you to all of you I have mentioned and the countless others I could not fit within these few pages. You all served so very well.

Thank you!

Index

About the Author

Bob Livingston is a consummate client service professional, schooled in over 40 years of interactions with clients and customers. Success has fueled his passion for service, while experience has earned him the respect of colleagues as a learned advocate for exceptional client service. It was this experience that formed his beliefs and provided the content in this book.

His career took form at the Lipton Tea Company, a multibillion-dollar subsidiary of Unilever and one of the world's leading food manufacturers. His leadership of their very large sales organization produced widely recognized client relationships that stand to this day.

After Lipton, Bob joined The Nielsen Company as a full-time advisor, and for a period of time he led their client service organization. He still serves as a consultant to Nielsen on client service matters and moderates their client advisory boards, giving him access and exposure to just about every major supplier and retailer in the consumer products industry. His passion for service has been conveyed broadly to thousands of client service professionals throughout his career in the form of personal interactions, seminars, and keynote addresses.

Bob currently leads REL Communications Inc., a consulting firm that works with companies to guide their client teams in the development of client relationship strategies. His personal experiences with some of the world's preeminent brands and consumer packaged goods companies form the foundation for this book. Those experiences have been further enhanced by his connection to hundreds of other consumer and retailer brands through years of industry and client associations.

For additional information on personal or company service transformations, please visit www.relcommunications.com or contact Bob Livingston at bob@relcommunications.com.

For seminar and keynote information and availability contact:
Tom Neilssen
BrightSight Group
609-924-3060
tom@brightsightgroup.com